Writer's Craft, Teacher's Art

WRITER'S CRAFT, TEACHER'S ART

Teaching What We Know

Edited by
MIMI SCHWARTZ
Stockton State College

BOYNTON/COOK PUBLISHERS
HEINEMANN
Portsmouth, NH

Boynton/Cook Publishers, Inc.
A Subsidiary of
Heinemann Educational Books, Inc.
361 Hanover Street, Portsmouth, NH 03801
Offices and agents throughout the world

The following have generously given permission to use quotations
from copyrighted work:

"Dolor," copyright © 1943 by Modern Poetry Association, Inc. From
The Collected Poems of Theodore Roethke by Theodore Roethke. Used by
permission of Doubleday, a division of Bantam, Doubleday, Dell
Publishing Group, Inc.

Every effort has been made to contact the copyright holders and
students for permission to reprint borrowed material. We regret any
oversights that may have occurred and would be happy to rectify
them in future printings of this work.

Library of Congress Cataloging-in-Publication Data
Writer's craft, teacher's art : teaching what we know / edited by Mimi
   Schwartz.
        p.   cm.
     Includes bibliographical references.
     ISBN 0-86709-263-7
     1. English language—Rhetoric—Study and teaching. I. Schwartz,
Mimi.
PE1404.W675   1990
808'.042'07—dc20   90-37593
                                                              CIP

Front-cover photo by Wladislaw Finne
Designed by Wladislaw Finne
Printed in the United States of America
91 92 93 94 95   10 9 8 7 6 5 4 3 2 1

Contents

Acknowledgments

Every contributor to this book deserves a thanks here. For in addition to their individual essays, they generously provided—by phone and mail—feedback on each other's work. As a result, everyone had several readers for work in progress. My special thanks to Kim Stafford for suggesting the title, to Ken Autrey for his advice on how to be an editor and on the introduction, and to Peter Stillman for guiding me through the process. Finally, my thanks to Stu Schwartz, a professor of engineering and my husband, who was willing to listen, read, and give advice—even over morning coffee.

Introduction

This book began on Martha's Vineyard three years ago, with this question: "How many of you consider yourself writers?" I was teaching a two-week seminar on writing to twenty-five writing teachers from twenty states, mostly from English departments but also from economics, psychology, and math. Two hands went up. "What about the rest of you?" I asked, somewhat surprised because most of what I teach about writing comes out of my experience as a writer. "You've all been writing since you were six. Why not?"

"We're not good enough...famous enough...creative enough. ...What we write—memos, letters, articles, reports, diaries, grants—that doesn't count," said the Noes. (The Yesses, who hadn't published much more, felt, as I did, that it did count.)

"Then how do you convince your students that *they* are writers? Why should they believe you?" I wanted to know. Only twenty minutes before, when discussing current theories of teaching writing, everyone had agreed that students did need to *feel* like writers in order to write well. It gave them the commitment and confidence to carry on. No question about it.

What worried me about these right-minded convictions was that they were based on the latest paradigms and handbooks— but not on experience. Even a good theory develops rigor mortis under such conditions and—like the mother who doesn't swim, trying to coax her child into the water—it won't work. What our profession needed, I realized, both in perception and in the literature, was more connection between practice and pedagogy, between teaching and writing.

Hence, the genesis of this book. The premise of *Writer's Craft, Teacher's Art* is that teachers *are* writers, that what we do on a yellow pad or at a word processor—whether it's a memo or a poem—affects what we teach about writing. The book's purpose is to explore this connection, so that as a profession we come to see teacher and writer not as two isolated roles but as one interrelated one.

To accomplish this, sixteen writer/teachers who do both regularly—poets, journalists, economists, fiction writers, physicists, and English professors—join me in describing the connections between how we write and teach. Collectively, we represent a broad range of writing experiences (from prize-winning poetry to memos to the President) and teaching experiences (from freshman comp at Harvard to tech writing at Arkansas). And we cover a variety of issues in composing, from writer's block to revision and assessment, based not on theory but on firsthand experience with high school deadlines, *Cosmo* editors, department colleagues, or picky dissertation committees.

These essays are conversational in tone, with a strong personal voice, so you can know the person behind the words. This is true not only for essays involving memoir, such as Stephen Tchudi's "Confessions of a Failed Bookmaker" and Andy Herrmann's "Anxious, B-L-O-C-K-E-D, and Computer Phobic: A Writing Teacher's Memoirs," but also for cross-disciplinary dialogues such as Charles Moran's and Bill Mullin's "Dialogue Across the Two Cultures" and essays about research such as my "Teaching What We Know About Revision." We all share one goal: to keep the "I" permanently on center stage, rhetorically and thematically, both to narrate our stories *and* to present the theories and practices that emerged from them.

It was a challenge to do both without letting the seams of *exposition* show—particularly for academic writers, who, unlike the poets and fiction writers, are used to bifurcating their voices: academic for one occasion, personal for another. But it can be done, as Gabriele Rico's opening essay illustrates. She moves in one paragraph from personal experience

> *In minutes I had drafted something that* felt *right—the first time I genuinely felt like a "real" writer. . . . It was a moment of profound pleasure. Something was right, yet the questions persisted. . . .*

to brain research on creativity without missing a beat:

> *During this time of creative turmoil, I rediscovered in my files a passage from Brewster Ghiselin's introduction to* The Creative

Process (1952). He had written: "Chaos and disorder are perhaps the wrong terms for that indeterminate fullness and activity...."

We all tried to follow suit, but this naturalness was often hard-earned, involving feedback (we exchanged drafts) and revisions to keep our personal voice steady—in exposition as well as narrative. The above lines, for example, in Rico's earlier version were more stilted:

In the ensuing years, a passage of Brewster Ghiselin's introduction to The Creative Process *(1952) frequently floated into my consciousness....*

"I feel as if I'm making a translation," says Linda Nelson, whose essay "On Writing My Way Home" describes her conflict in reconciling public and private voice within the academic establishment. It is a struggle we all dealt with, in trying to find an authentic voice for presenting the mix of ideas and personal experience.

It is a struggle that also belongs in our classrooms. Students, too, need to learn how to bridge the rhetorical gap, often vast for them, between the occasional personal narrative (usually a warm-up assignment) and argumentative essays, which are the meat and potatoes of academic writing. We hope our essays provide some 1990 examples of what Montaigne, father of the essay, knew in 1580: that the personal need not negate the intellectual and that, as Phillip Lopate points out in "What Happened to the Personal Essay?" (in *Against Joie de Vivre*, Poseidon Press, 1989), there wasn't always "an un-Montaignean split between the formal and informal essay."

Writer's Craft, Teacher's Art is divided into three sections that reflect different perspectives concerning practice and pedagogy. The first, "Strategies," deals with techniques we rely on most heavily as writers: to get started, to revise, to read meaningfully, to gather information, to take risks, to address different audiences. The second, "Insights," presents some lessons that we have learned from others—editors, writing groups, newspaper critics, teachers, and mentors. These people, good and bad, have helped to shape our attitudes and responses as writers and teachers. The third, "Dilemmas," defines some of the ongoing conflicts that we face concerning creativity, competence versus excellence, writer's block, the lack of time, finding an authentic voice, and how much of our conflicts we should share with students.

You'll find common refrains in our essays about how writing has shaped our teaching: the value of practicing what you preach; the importance of more personalized writing in school; the danger of overbearing rules, both to creativity and confidence; and most important, the need to treat writers, at all levels, with respect for what they are *trying* to say—whether it is working or not. These beliefs, rooted in individual experience, point to our collective needs as writers—teachers and students alike—if we are to *feel* like writers. Making connections between how we write and teach helps to keep us honest, by reminding us deep down of what these needs are.

I

STRATEGIES

...teaching what we do as prewriters, revisers, eavesdroppers, researchers, risk-takers, etc.

1

Writer:
Personal Patterns
in Chaos

GABRIELE RICO

Gabriele Rico has just ended a year-long sabbatical from San Jose State University and is now completing **Pain and Possibility: Writing Your Way through Personal Crisis.** *When she isn't writing, she is teaching an experimental humanities course entitled "Paths to the Present: Spirit of Enlightenment and Revolution" and a graduate seminar in composition. When she isn't teaching, she lectures widely on creativity, the brain, and learning. Author of the best-selling* **Writing the Natural Way** *and holder of a Stanford Ph.D., she is excited about her newly proposed interdisciplinary seminar "Creative Process and Chaos Theory."*

Writer. What an awesome word it was to me, an eighteen-year-old undeclared English major! The word conjured up Shakespeare and Shelley, Montaigne and Melville, Hemingway and Hopkins, Woolf and Wolfe—actually, whatever writers I was attached to at the moment. These "real" writers had succeeded in an impossible dream: to cover pages with poems, fill notebooks with novels or plays, compose essays that were *really* their own.

I loved their cadences, their metaphors, their images; I loved their passion, producing passionate feelings in me as I read.

Writer. I knew the word did not apply to me; inside my head was a chaos I could not untangle in my own words; I was only a cutter and paster, a borrower, a fake. While real writers shaped form and content, I felt little more than a hopelessly tangled fullness where ideas should be. Although I managed to write my analyses, term papers, examinations, I felt little pleasure in my words on a page, little passion for writing, despite my love of reading.

Teacher. At twenty-one I stood before a class, teaching the prescribed think-schemes so useful since Aristotle. Following these instructional schemata gave me a sense of security, but they were neither satisfying nor effective. Discouraged, I consoled myself: "Not everyone is meant to write. Look at their performances!" And it was true: the A students at the beginning of the course remained the A students at the end; the C students at the beginning stayed C students at the end; and at the bottom there was the motley crew whose efforts were so garbled they could never rise above the fatal F. They were not writers!

Writer? When I was twenty-four, a professor asked me to write an article for the *English Journal* about my approach to teaching poetry. Honored, I signed up for two units of special study, then agonized, made innumerable false starts, tried an outline, became intolerably anxious. I felt a chaotic fullness of ideas, but I didn't know where to start, what to say, how to say it. My unexpressed ideas went the way of an incomplete, which I finally—and guiltily—let slide into an F. At last, the evidence was incontrovertible: I was no writer, either! My sense of inadequacy had become a self-fulfilling prophesy. How, I wondered, *how* can ordinary students ever feel like writers when I, approaching a Master's degree in English, didn't, couldn't? Something was wrong; something was missing.

Time passed, and I found myself once more a student, this time in a Stanford doctoral program. Writing was hard, but I gritted my teeth and plowed ahead. During those exhilarating and difficult years, I became aware of odd moments in which the less I plowed, the more the words flowed. I had only inklings, but these moments seemed to coincide with a tacit rejection of what I taught. I began to pay attention. The flow seemed to be triggered only when I gave myself over to that disconcerting, chaotic fullness inside my head, acknowledged the untidy, sideways leaps of thought, let go of logic and prescriptions. I liked the feeling, although it came all too rarely, like dreams of flying that cannot be forced. How to trigger this flow? The question began to preoccupy me.

In 1973 an essay on creativity and the brain by split-brain pioneer Joseph Bogen (1973) produced an epiphany: the mind was anything but a straight thinker. It was permissible to feel muddled instead of logical, to produce outlines only after a paper was finished, to table the accepted think-schemes in favor of allowing something less definable, more organic to emerge. This new meta-awareness changed, in profound ways, how I write, how I teach, how I perceive my students' potential.

Through my doctoral work, the untidy, irregular process of clustering was born. Embarrassingly simple, it made the silent, invisible processes of the mind's search for meaningful patterns visible on the page. It was a mind-tool to capture the mind's odd, unruly, a-logical leaps; it revealed unexpected connections radiating from a center in all directions. The resulting writing came unbidden, and I recalled E. M. Forster's famous imperative "Only connect!" I was astonished at what my students produced. All levels, from top to bottom writers, seemed able to tap into an internal organizing process from which they wrote readily and with pleasure. An example from those early days is the product of a highly reluctant "bottom writer." Fear of failing yet once more paralyzed her. "Try clustering just once," I urged, circling the word GREEN on her paper. In five minutes she had produced the following cluster and vignette:

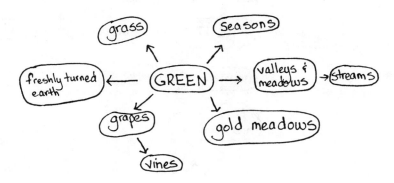

Green valleys and gold meadows. Warm orange pumpkins.
Grapes on a vine. Dew glistens on unmowed grass. Fish swim in

lakes of silver. The smell of freshly turned earth. Seasons are but four. Green is the time of life.

She glowed. I knew I had something. In a few minutes she had drafted a cohesive whole—despite its fragments. As she began to trust the flow and see its evidence spread before her on the page, her confidence grew with every writing task. I, for my part, began to experiment in earnest by searching for trigger words and images, ranging from adjectives to prepositions, proverbs to paintings, physical objects to names. Students invariably produced highly compressed, almost poetic, vignettes with great fluency. Something was right; something was happening, and much of it had to do with a sense of pleasure and satisfaction, with valuing the act of being expressive through language instead of associating it with force and formula.

Shifting to the visual arts, I asked students to come up with their own center by naming a dominant impression and clustering around it. In choosing a Jackson Pollock painting, I recall thinking, "If they can create their own meaning from this, something important is going on." A Freshman "middle" writer saw FRENZY clustered, then wrote, all in less than ten minutes:

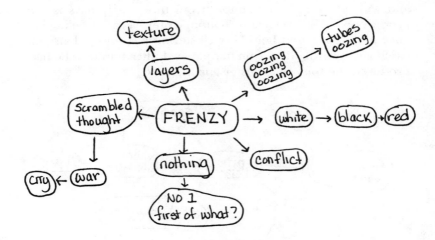

I see his movements. He is entranced by his own creative frenzy. He frantically swirls his arms over the canvas, squeezing tubes of pigment, dashing from one end to the other. The paint oozes, drips, splashes onto the white surface below. Black, then white, then a

splash of red, then more black. The layers pile on, one on top of the other. I sit still and watch him work. I wonder what he is thinking. Sweat pours from his forehead. Is he thinking of his life? The war? The city? The traffic? I don't know. I see only his movement. The canvas comes alive with movement. The painting is movement. J.T.

For me, teaching composition became ongoing research and discovery instead of drudgery. The mounting evidence of varied and vital vignettes, even from our least able students, convinced me that, over the years, we had unwittingly put the cart before the horse by beginning with the think-schemes so self-evident to us. In so doing, we had scotched a fundamental human need: student-as-creator first; writing, first and foremost, as a self-organizing act. And we were disappointed when too few students could measure up to the prescriptions, which largely ignored the fact that composing, especially in its initial stages, is an organic process having little to do with think-schemes:

Correctness, in the end, is desirable, but placing it before the creation of meaning is confusing the means with the ends of writing, like hitting the right notes but missing the melody. (Source unknown)

And so it was. In my early struggles to teach composition I was hitting a lot of right notes but missing the melody. Clustering became a means to evoke each mind's unique melody-making potential, a mind-tool for making those emergent melodies visible on a clean white page. My doctoral work on metaphoric thought (1976) documented the rationale for and the effects of clustering. *Writing the Natural Way,* the result of several years' experimentation to discover what happened naturally without traditional instruction, was published in 1982. So much for history. So much for students.

So little for me. I still didn't *feel* like a writer, did not risk writing with my students for those few minutes each day. One day, in yet another experiment, I wrote TOUCH/FEEL on the board. Scanning my students' absorbed faces focused on some inner melody, I suddenly wanted to hear it, too. Writing TOUCH/FEEL on a page, I felt the familiar, anxiety-provoking sense of chaos. This time, instead of staving it off by stopping, I moved toward it, flowed into it. Words, phrases, images, lines of poems spilled out around the center, making their own indecipherable pattern. After a minute or so of clustering, I experienced a shift from a sense of randomness to a sense of direction, pattern, flow. I began to write:

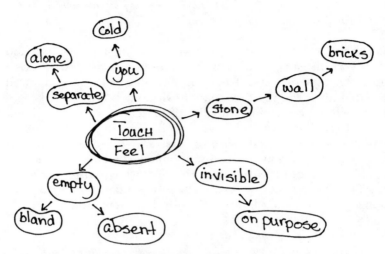

After Eighteen Years of Marriage
(For R.)

The stone wall around your mind—
built one by one to keep me
from touching you—
I feel.
I tap and tap but cannot touch.
You are invisible in your stone prison,
empty as air, not there.

I am lost in your invisibility:
Invisibility by absence;
inside your stone wall is a vacant lot.
Invisibility by blandness;
you blend into neutrality of feeling—
I cannot reach you.
Invisibility by design;
you calculate its effects.

Stopped cold by stone,
I cannot break through—
turn invisible, too,
empty as air, not there.

When I looked up, five minutes had passed; it could have been five seconds, five hours. I had been swept up by a distant melody of feeling-tones that became more distinct as I wrote. In minutes I had drafted something that *felt* right—the first time I genuinely *felt* like a "real" writer. Clustering had *in*-volved me in the discovery of an inner pattern, which had *e*-volved into a design of words on a page. It was a moment of profound pleasure. Something was very right, yet I still had no language for this experience. Although my deep involvement with brain research had helped me make a 180 degree turnaround in my teaching, I was still searching for a better way to talk about that shift. I knew the erratic nature of creative process had much to do with the sense of chaos I had always perceived as a negative.

During this time of creative turmoil, I rediscovered in my files a passage from Brewster Ghiselin's introduction to *The Creative Process* (1952):

> *Chaos and disorder are perhaps the wrong terms for that indeterminate fullness and activity of the inner life. For it is organic, dynamic, full of tension and tendency. . . . It is a working sea of indecision, but if it were altogether without structure of some kind it would be without life.*

Was he speaking of the same chaos that for me had conjured up only negative images of formlessness, absence of order, utter anarchy? For Ghiselin, chaos was an "indeterminate fullness," a "tension and tendency," a "sea of indecision" nevertheless in some way "organic, dynamic." Yes! Yes! I knew that feeling! This paradox recalled Wallace Stevens's lines:

> *In Chaos and his song is a consolation.*
> *It is the music of the mass of meaning. (p. 256)*

Yes. Chaos had melody. Yes! In some strange way, Chaos was "the music of the mass of meaning." Yes. These two passages echoed in my mind like a vaguely familiar melody. Yes. Perhaps *chaos* was a good word after all for that sense of fullness in my head that had seemed worthless at best, terrifying at worst.

Not until 1986, when I stumbled upon James Gleick's *Chaos: Making a New Science*, did I perceive a whole web of connections between my long-standing interests in brain function, creative process, the nonlinear correspondences of metaphor, and in my own writing rigidity, my students' general dislike of writing, and Ghiselin's and Stevens's passages on chaos. Since then, Chaos theory has guided much of my current work.

For me, the science of Chaos has become a powerful analogue for the nonlinearity of human consciousness, for creative process, for honoring the tenuous sense of melody *before* focusing on its notes. In science, Chaos is a short-hand name for ways of processing the irregular, the discontinuous, erratic side of nature not explainable by classical science. In fact, the Science of Chaos begins where classical science leaves off, reflecting the discovery of delicate, recursive structures underlying complexity, such as crashing waves, jagged coastlines, tree-shapes repeated in unpredictable ways in their leaf-shapes. *Chaos* is the science of open rather than closed systems; as such it is neither random nor codifiable, rather a complex interaction of irregular but recursive patterns. These patterns in chaos became accessible through two events: (1) the mathematician Benoit Mandelbrot (Gleick, p. 98) invented a new form of mathematics called "fractal geometry," which reveals irregular, recursive patterns in chaos, not random behavior at all, for example, the recursiveness in a coastline seen from a jet to ever smaller *fractals* thereof—a bay, a jagged boulder, a microscopic look at a grain of sand (Hooper and Teresi, p. 373). (2) The new capabilities of the computer transformed these fractal equations into astonishingly beautiful filigrees (see below). The new science that produced these images is rich

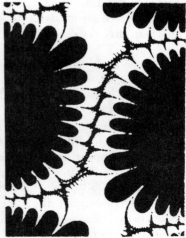

in implications for the strange "tension and tendency" of the mind's creative process—and, by extension, the writing process.

The generative power of Chaos theory suggests that writing is anything but sequential; it is much more like fractal mind-leaps, irregularly expanding orbits. The process of clustering reflects these irregular, sideways-leaping, roundabout processes described by Chaos theory. Seeming randomness and the resonance of potential melody are simultaneously made manifest on the page. If the human mind is indeed an open system, clustering becomes the visible reflection of its dynamic, recursive, self-organizing capability for spontaneous emergent activity. And that is precisely what happens with clustering: although it initially feels random, the mind discovers patterns in chaos. In the seemingly chance choices we discover recursiveness; in the radical irregularities of thought-leaps, we become aware of patterns of meaning that we did not conceive of before. Poet William Stafford describes this process powerfully:

It is like fishing. But I do not wait very long, for there is always a nibble—and this is where receptivity comes in. To get started I will accept anything that occurs to me. Something always occurs, of course, to any of us. We can't keep from thinking. Maybe I have to settle for an immediate impression: it's cold, or hot, or dark, or bright, or in between! Or—well, the possibilities are endless. If I put down something, that thing will help the next thing come, and I'm off. If I let the process go on, things will occur to me that were not at all in my mind when I started. These things, odd or trivial as they may be, are somehow connected.

Observing the "somehow connected" aspect of the mind's odd leaps in clustering after years of collecting and analyzing students' resulting spontaneous writing is precisely what attracted me to Chaos theory: it has clarified for me that learning receptivity is not an option but an imperative. Becoming receptive to that chaotic fullness of mind instead of fearing or suppressing it leads to expressive word patterns that rarely cease to surprise. Herein lies the key to feeling like a writer—receptivity to chaos as absolute potential. It has little to do with being famous or published and much to do with the difference between flow and force. "Writers" give themselves permission to flow with the mind's chaos before attempting to force order on something not yet orderable. As composition teachers we have understandably sought to simplify such apparent disorder by imposing rules from without at the expense of possible patterns from within. Our think-schemes have their rightful place but only after experiencing awareness of the intricate webs of the mind's chaos from the inside out. M. C. Richards has observed: "It is difficult to stand forth in one's growing, if one is not permitted to live through the stages of one's unripeness, clumsiness, unreadiness, as well as one's grace and aptitude" (p 40).

And that describes clustering: it permits receptivity to the "tension and tendency" of the mind's rich and resonant chaos, allowing the discovery of personal meaning. Let me illustrate with a second vignette that would have been impossible for me to produce in my "forcing" mode. My students and I were clustering the generic PERSON as an experiment in imaging. I was picturing relatives, acquaintances, fictional characters, clustering names rapidly, becoming receptive to flow. With an emotional jolt, I stopped with my youngest daughter's name. An unmistakeable pattern! I placed SIMONE in a second circle and reclustered, curious to see where this pattern would lead. It was not long before the following emerged unbidden:

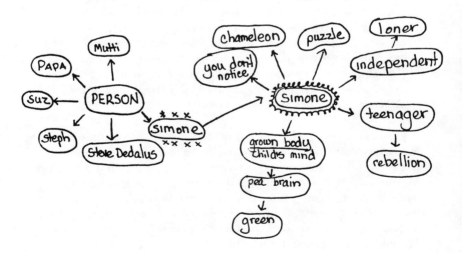

For Simone

Your own one-child-show at three,
you played hour on hour, alone with non-existent toys,

imaginary friends, talking mice, building whole villages
in the fertile soil of the Sierra campground.
You grew into full-breasted sullenness too soon,
determined to unravel—all alone—the center of your being.
YOU were grown—you green-pea, pea-brain, princess on a pea—
demanded I see you for yourself, accused:
"You don't notice me!"
  I didn't,
    absorbed in my own fears and failures.

Wise one, foolish one, youngest one, my puzzle, my magic trick,
my chameleon, where are you going, going . . .
When will you be gone?
And how will you come back?

The unsuspected, certainly unexpressed, ambivalence toward
this teenager, translated into words on the page, shocked me,
and later became a vehicle for sharing with her—though that is
another story. What is important here is that my receptivity to
my own emotional chaos led organically to flow. Now, almost
always, I am surprised by what my receptivity to chaos produces.
As teacher I have grasped the imperative of letting my students
feel the potential of their chaos before attempting to impose my
order.

My own experience with trusting chaos informs my teaching
of writing. By letting students learn to be receptive to their
mind's chaos, they will learn to express their own awkward melodies first, derive pleasure from the swiftness and relative sim-
plicity by which they take shape. Only then can they feel like
writers; and only then can they become willing editors of the
notes that comprise their melodies. Only when students can actually experience the pleasure that comes from shaping emergent patterns can they even come close to Einstein's definition
of the aesthetic, which he said has two components: the first is
the creation of what one perceives as a whole; the second is the
sense of profound satisfaction that comes from having created
that whole.

In evoking writing, I have come to value the compression of
the poetic before the expansion of the expository, to engage the
feeling dimension before logic. Clustering has led my surprised

students to metaphoric leaps, to awareness of language rhythms, to recurring patterns of images, words, phrases, sounds, in fact, to many of the stylistic devices we associate largely with "top" writers but which tend to come naturally to all writers when they are listening for their own melodies first, critiquing the notes that comprise their melodies second. Students will undergo significant changes in attitude and skill, even without formal instruction (error rates usually drop by 50 percent when students write from a cluster). They develop a sense of ownership in the products they have a genuine stake in. Without this sense of personal involvement and permission to risk, most students will never see themselves as writers.

The empowerment inherent in flowing rather than forcing is virtually immediate. In my classes, a daily, five-minute *Thought-log*, from which the following examples are taken, lets students practice flow. An adult reentry student clusters CARE, and in five minutes writes her way through a metaphoric leap about human verbal behavior.

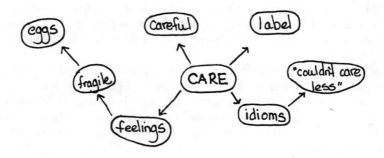

I often wonder if the phrase, "I couldn't care less" isn't often a verbal survival package. We box our most delicate feelings in conventional covers, like egg cartons, carefully constructed to cushion its fragile contents.

An eighteen-year-old responds to the trigger FRAGMENTS, resulting in a playful vignette that demonstrates considerable understanding of sentence structure and punctuation.

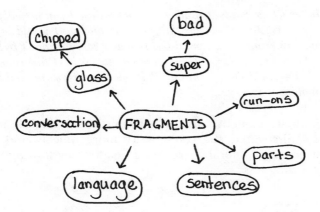

What's wrong with writing. In fragments. Fragments are short. Consise. And powerful. They beat run-on sentences by a mile don't you agree? Run-on sentences tend to go on forever without end like space they're useless and directionless. But fragments are short. With a definite beginning. And end. I fail to see. What is wrong. With using fragments.

An eighteen-year-old special-admit student, whose diagnostic essay was so garbled it was virtually unreadable, clustered RANDOM and, in eight minutes, produced a vignette expressive of a dawning meta-awareness of his own awareness.

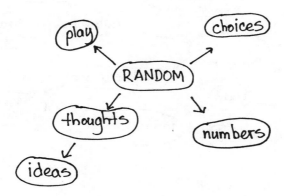

Cluster let me think at random. I can't believe I can actually sit and write. Writing is the one thing I never thought I would like to do, but clustering lets my mind feel free and easy so I don't feel tied down to writing on something I have no interest in. Clustering lets me talk to myself about meanings that come into my mind and frees my inhibitions to write.

A graduate student, already a sophisticated English major "writer," discovered she could write more quickly and with greater economy, literally stretching her time by flowing more and agonizing less.

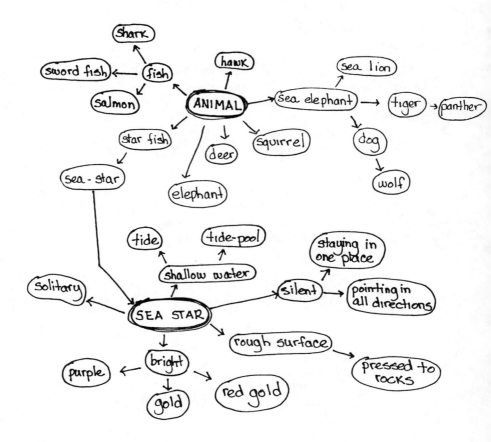

I, My Animal
The rough purple arch of my back glows,
bright splash against dark rocks.

I suck the sand, foam, water—
  stretch my salt-slicked arms
  pointing in all directions
while hulk and bulk of my soul
hunches in secret,
clinging to a single,
smooth place on the rock.

Giving you directions,
I remain unmoved.
I stay still with my silence
where I can absorb and interpret
vibrations of water, changes in tide.

Fed full with my silence,
I am alone
  carrying the center of my solitude
  in the skin of a star.

                Lisa Ricks

The final example stems from a *Thoughtlog* entry that had an emotional impact so strong for the writer that he chose to develop it into a formal paper with its own unique, clearly developed narrative structure.

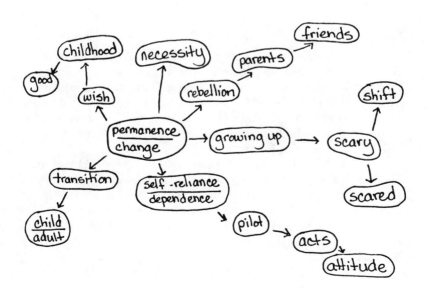

In Transition

I feel I don't fit anymore. My friends, my buddies, even my girl-friend all went away to college. I'm the only one left of our "gang." I am lonely, tired, and so old. Sometimes I feel like the ancient street-man who walks down Lincoln Avenue with two canes, bent, spent. These are the best years of my life? I worry about the future. My apprehensions are based on my inexperience in making major decisions which will affect my life in major ways.

My parents had my life completely planned for me. I really dis-appointed them when I announced I didn't want to follow the blueprints. When nothing seems to fit anymore, a transition is inev-itable. Things that don't alter are discarded. Dinosaurs could not adapt to a changing environment. Now they are extinct.

But what of me? I am a grounded pilot. I am a cat with a bell around my neck—the birds know where I am. I used to try living up to standards set by other people. Suddenly I saw that I need to live by my own standards. I can actually feel the changes in myself, in my attitude, in my actions. I am moving into a transition period. I am shifting from boyhood to manhood, from security to indepen-dence, from reliance on others to self-sufficiency.

Unfortunately for me, this transition feels like shifting without a clutch. I am a lynx on the banks of a great river, pacing. Behind me the fire rages, huge, terrifying, and hot. Once I leap I cannot turn back. My whiskers begin to singe. I jump.

This student's writing gained power because he became re-ceptive to the conflicting feelings of his simultaneous desire for, and fear of, asserting his independence. The sense of confusion evolved into metaphors that allowed him, for the first time, to articulate his feelings; his weeks of writing brief vignettes at the beginning of each class hour enabled him to trust his chaos, to risk a real voice in a longer paper.

Once students become receptive to their mind's chaos, they become willing riskers, receptive learners, willing shapers of products they have an emotional stake in. When, at the end of each semester, I ask students to respond to "Writing is..." as their final entry, their shift in attitude is palpable; it breathes through their words, dances in their sentences, sings their honesty.

Writing is discovering and uncovering what goes on inside of you. What you remember. What you forgot. Writing is revealing yourself to yourself in the same way that you become intimate with someone who was once a stranger. Writing is difficult because it depends on exposure of yourself to the one who thinks most critically of you—yourself. Writing is bizarre when it is finished and you step back and say, "Did I write that?!" Writing is selfish because it can be what you most care about, and others may not understand. Writing is fun because you finally use one of the seldom-tapped resources of your mind. Writing is necessary.

Eighteen-year-old freshman

I learned from my students that I had the right to the name "writer" after all—after all the years of not measuring up to some external standard, but only after learning to respect my own patterns in chaos, my own melodies, my own voice. I now know the meaning of William Stafford's manifesto of the human being as creator, that

writing is one of the great free human activities. There is scope for individuality, and elation, and discovery. In writing, for the person who follows with trust and forgiveness what occurs to him, the world remains always ready and deep, an inexhaustible environment.

That "inexhaustible environment" has its roots in the fertile chaos of mind. Trust it.

WORKS CITED

Bogen, Joseph E. "The Other Side of the Brain: An Appositional Mind." *The Nature of Human Consciousness.* Ed. Robert Ornstein. San Francisco: W. H. Freeman, 1973.

Ghiselin, Brewster, ed. *The Creative Process.* New American Library, 1952.

Gleick, James. *Chaos: Making a New Science.* New York: Viking, 1987.

Hooper, Judith and Dick Teresi, *The 3-Pound Universe.* N.Y.: Macmillan Pub. Co., 1987.

Richards, M. C. *Centering: Poetry, Pottery, and the Person.* Middletown, CT: Wesleyan UP, 1962.

Rico, Gabriele. *Metaphor and Knowing: Analysis, Synthesis, Rationale.* Diss. Stanford U, 1976.

Rico, Gabriele. *Writing the Natural Way.* Los Angeles: Jeremy P. Tarcher/St. Martin's, 1982.

Stafford, William. *Writing the Australian Crawl: Views on the Writer's Vocation.* Ann Arbor, MI: The University of Michigan Press, 1978.

Stevens, Wallace. *The Collected Poems of Wallace Stevens.* New York: Knopf, 1982.

2

Another Way of Writing: The Writer/Teacher as Professional Eavesdropper

KIM R. STAFFORD

Kim R. Stafford is Director of the Northwest Writing Institute of Lewis and Clark College in Portland, Oregon. He is the author of **Having Everything Right: Essays of Place,** *which won a citation for excellence from the Western State Book Award in 1986. He is also editor of a collection of folklore,* **Rendezvous: Stories, Songs, and Opinions of the Idaho Country.** *Currently, Stafford is working on a book about old growth forests and on another collection of essays,* **Where Everything Changes: Human Customs at the Margin of the Wilderness.**

As a free-wheeling writer of personal essays, I hold a dark secret: I was once a medievalist, a scholar. I once haunted libraries, pored over glossaries, thumbed my *Beowulf* and my *Pearl* to rags. I have written twenty pages on the use of the feminine pronoun in a single stanza of an obscure poem from the fourteenth century; I have worked sleepless through nights to dawn, heating cold rooms with the sheer stamina of my reading. I have internalized the nuances of suffixes in ancient texts so that I can recite what I no longer understand. That was a long and wonderful training for something I don't do now.

Now that I write, what do I do with that training? Now that I teach writing, how does my scholarship pertain? For both writing and teaching, I now turn that tireless scholarly attention to the flow of language that surrounds me in the world. I read talk. I annotate conversation. I catalog graffiti. I favor the traveler's fictions in bus stations, the whispered confessions of the midnight lounge car on the train. I long for the banter of hitchhikers listing their rides and destinations, the semi-public narratives of small cafes. I scribble and study conversations at the twenty-four hour Elkhorn Cafe in Jackson Hole; I record fictions spoken at the Burns Brothers Truck Plaza south from Portland. I take the corner booth, hunch over my coffee, and listen two ways. I fit my elbows to the twin worn spots at the counter, and tune in at the frayed periphery of my hearing. I give to speeches flaunted at the Acropolis Diner in Brooklyn the attention I once reserved for the annual publications of the Early English Text Society.

I live in the modern world, but my habits are old ones. In the medieval period, books were so rare they were memorized. Travelers took turns reciting favorite texts. The feast of stories exchanged by the pilgrim band in Chaucer's *Canterbury Tales* exaggerates a social custom that was actual. The first book with pagination didn't appear until the fifteenth century; people *knew* the books they owned. Chaucer's contemporary John Gower apparently had eight books in his personal library; he had memorized all eight, and he wove quotations from them throughout his work. But as Socrates had warned his students, once we learn to read we will forget how to remember. Gutenberg imprisoned literature, and schools maintain the tyranny. How can we join the world again—the medieval permanent human world of literature alive in public life?

One chill morning I was walking across my college campus, in haste for the fall convocation, when I passed two maintenance workers sunk hip-deep in a ditch to repair a steam pipe. Mud covered their feet, steam hissed about their heads, and one said to the other as I passed, "As the world grows colder around us, sincerity and honesty must be the fire to keep us warm." I smiled with pleasure, savoring this literature of the street, and went on, head down, to work. But then I stopped abruptly. On the steps to the auditorium, I took out the tiny notebook I always carry in my heart-pocket to write such sentences down. I would hear, or read, or invent nothing better for some days. Sincerity and honesty—how could I live by these? How could I write and teach by these?

Some of my colleagues in the language-rich professions of teaching and writing admit they overhear such occasional gems, but they often explain them away.

"Those maintenance workers were probably some of our English majors," said a colleague, "who couldn't get real jobs."

"Yeah, *sure* you heard that!" said another.

"Did you make that up?"

What is this cynicism about language, and about humanity? Genius lives where the language lives. Some witness it, overhearing by chance; I do so professionally. I do so because eavesdropping makes of life a perpetual feast, and because I'm not often smart enough as a writer to invent things as good as what I hear. Another way to say that may be more honest: by listening to the glories of conversations around me, I'm reminded to listen to my own furtive thoughts and dreams. In their inventive talk, my wise neighbors give me permission to take seriously my own private voice.

In my experience, pleasure in writing begins with a sense of abundance—abundant knowledge and boundless curiosity. A student writer, or a professional journalist, can get by without abundance, but cannot thrive. Yes, anyone can begin with just enough information to fill a required writing assignment. Writing can feel like an examination. Or it can feel like flight. I anchor that feeling of abundance in the fat little notebook in my pocket. I urge my students to study the hum of talk around them, and to bring overheard fragments to class so we may revel together. I urge them to attend to the common muse. I love Chaucer, but Chaucer is not my muse. Published literature is not my muse. For the muses are all around us. They seem ordinary but are very busy, very generous. I listen everywhere, hush my companion when a good story drifts into range, pull out my notebook, and smile.

"I'll tell you later," I whisper.

I make my notebooks two and three-quarters by four and a quarter inches, from three sheets of paper folded, slit, and sewn into brown coverstock with black thread flavored with beeswax. The little book is a plain and fragrant object. I fold it open to the next fresh page, and slip it into my shirt pocket. I make up a dozen notebooks at a time, stick an address label on the inside cover of each, and date them as I begin. On the outside cover I put a stamp, usually that old one-center with the pen and inkwell that proclaims, "The ability to write—a root of democracy." Such a notebook lasts me about a week. Every few months, I sit down with a stack of notebooks and glean the best stories, sayings, and thoughts, and I file these with my dozen essays in progress.

My own writing routine surges in a steady stream of notebooks, drafts, and essays. When I teach, I suggest my students catalog their eavesdropping into several key categories: (1) conversations overheard; (2) informal speeches; (3) written texts from the street; and (4) graffiti and short phrases. One might label sections of the notebook by these or similar categories, but in my own work I don't. I take it all down as it comes, and organize it later, selecting the best for current work and letting the rest undertake the yeasty work of time on the shelf, in the drawer, in my mind. From such external voices, my students and I move to eavesdropping on our own dreams and our daily, fleeting thoughts. In a way, I am an informal folklorist in the world and an eavesdropper on the self, and I encourage my students to conduct fieldwork on their own cultures and their own minds. We start by taking dictation from the world.

CONVERSATIONS OVERHEARD

In a cafe in San Antonio, I listened as two truck drivers discussed their route toward Houston. They talked about how to take the blue highways to get around the city, but still make good time. Then there was a quiet conversation I couldn't hear. After a pause, the young one spoke with conviction.

"You could call that the source of all knowledge. You could say 'self,' and be exact about all people." They talked quietly awhile, then the young one concluded aloud, "We don't create anything; we just integrate ourselves into all that is."

What does a writer do with such clues? Since I seek abundance, I wait. After several days in San Antonio, my notebook also contains a sermon by a priest at the Cathedral of San Fernando, a long midnight run of jive talk by a street musician on a bridge, a sales pitch from a hat merchant at the open air *mercado,* a conversation with a cop at the Riverwalk, and a host of other fragments. Ironically, I have gathered these texts while avoiding most sessions of the 1987 NCTE annual convention. The convention taught me so much about language and literature in a few stellar sessions I had to flee from the chrome chairs of Medina Level B and listen in the streets to the spoken language itself. From this abundance I have written a long letter to a friend, which will become an essay called "The Source of All Knowledge in San Antonio." Two years beyond the first quick notes to myself, I'm sending this essay to my agent.

Preparing to write that essay took a rich few days, and a lingering two years. But throughout life I find myself barraged with rich conversation. I was sitting in a bar in Philadelphia, late one November evening, when I took down this conversation from two regulars in the next booth:

"So, you're going to be a father—when?"

"March."

"You going to be a husband, too?"

"Don't know. Maybe summer."

"Maybe, huh? You don't know or she don't?"

"I don't."

"Ah!"

What can I do with that? The characterization strikes me as very rich, very concise. Because all questions are not answered, there is room for a story to grow.

There is a rich effervescence to the writing life as I savor the sentence I overheard at an education conference: "Our district went on an economy drive—we don't use margins anymore!" I savor the line I overheard on a plane out of Cheyenne: "Danielle Steele? Oh, she's okay if you're on a cruise and the pool is full." I savor the lament by the cop at the cafe, as he put on his hat to go out into the rain: "Well, I guess I better get out there and fight crime, and sin, and lust, and pestilence. I keep fighting, but I never win. Oh well—God! It's raining, too!"

What I do with such fragments, again, is wait. Either several conversations will group themselves naturally in my mind into some kind of constellation for an essay, or they will simply enrich my abiding pleasure in the language and whet my hearing for more.

INFORMAL SPEECHES

I sat on a stone bench outside the downtown library in my native city of Portland, Oregon, listening as a street musician named Gypsy Slim, who had camped between two shopping carts for some months, harangued the pedestrians.

"I been to college," he proclaimed to a woman who had paused to listen, "majored in physics, minored in philosophy, and all the scientists will tell you the temperate zone is the most healthy—regular seasons, hot and cold. But I don't care if it's house, job, creed, ethnic group, country, institution, or sex— they *all* try to stifle what *you* can be! You want to *know* what you can be? Get outside all those categories and have a look!" Then his saxophone wrangled the air and pigeons scattered, and his listeners mostly tossed quarters into his hat and moved on.

On my stone bench, I put down the book I had been reading, and took out my notebook to get Slim's list. It took him, the outsider, to tell us all something true about ourselves. How could I honor what he knew?

Several weeks later, he disappeared. Now it has been years, and the pedestrians walk freely up the north side of Taylor Street. I brooded over his words, repeated them to friends. Troubled by his passing, I wrote a poem called "Whatever Happened to Gypsy Slim?" The poem quotes his harangue. I wrote an essay called "Local Character," in which Slim's speech sets the keynote for a host of eccentrics teaching hard truths to the communities they inhabit. I wrote a short story called "A Dancer on Salmon Street," in which Gypsy Slim's words help an exile from office work change his life. Many heard him speak; I took it down, and I study it over by writing it again and again.

As a writer, I am aware of the ethical issues involved in taking texts from strangers. I take these issues seriously. If I can't find Gypsy Slim to ask his permission before quoting him, am I a thief? My students ask me this, and I ask myself. It would be very wrong to use Slim's words irresponsibly. It would also be wrong to ignore his words. I take the risk because I believe in what he said to all of us. Sometime my eavesdropping may get me in trouble. But if we don't listen, if we avoid the issue by borrowing only from books, we are all in trouble. We are all diminished.

Gypsy Slim's speech found its way into my writing. Other speeches haven't yet, but I live with their verve, their ready potential. Take the fervent editorial spoken by my neighbor at the counter of the Skyline Cafe in Powell, Wyoming: "Son, you can go down to the variety store and get yourself a little bitty alligator no bigger than a lead pencil, and feed it bits of hamburger every day for a hundred years and it won't grow at all, but you start giving it whole hamburger patties on a plate and it will turn into a goddamn monster overnight, and that's *just* what happened to our federal government!"

I accept this gift. It is one of the most ambitious, breathless sentences I know. It gives me permission to stretch and listen to the long sentences that rise in my own voice.

In the midst of some danger, I relish the airline flight attendant's dig as we descend through low clouds toward the ground: "Ladies and gentlemen, you may have noticed the Captain has turned on the 'No Smoking' sign. This is his way of signaling to us that he *has* found the airport."

WRITTEN TEXTS

There are private ways to publish. You can pay a printer to run your verse, and then hawk your own books, which some call vanity publishing. Or you can staple your work to telephone poles, which I call generosity.

In Tijuana I found a ballad nailed to a pole late one Halloween night. The song was called "Mi Tijuana Querida," a loving ballad to the city itself. I stood in the dim light taking that text down, including the sentence in small writing at the end, which I translated, "You can't pay for this—it is for you." In Brooklyn, I found an anti-war parody of a Frost poem glued to a lamp post, beginning, "Whose head this is, I think I know...." I transcribed the verses that hadn't been bitten away by sleet. In Portland, I lifted a letter pasted to the sidewalk by rain beside a pile of someone's earthly possessions flung from an apartment window. It began, "John—Don't call Uncle Sammy anymore...." It ended, "Work Work Work. Pray Pray Pray. Write letters. No Calls. Violet."

What shall I do with these texts? There is a privacy in them, and a sufficiency to the moment of finding them. But I also feel the impulse to listen to the lives behind them, be their courier. With these, I don't know yet. And I feel in this "not knowing yet" the excitement of the writing life. I have a trove that might glitter in the sunlight, but I keep it in the drawer for now, wishing to use it well, to write honestly, responsibly. Something in my life will tell me what to do.

As I rambled the little town of Bucoda, Washington, early one morning, I came across a junk store with two tremendous padlocks on the door, a maze of wires extending from the doorknob inside, and a message spray-painted silver on the front wall: "LOCKS ELECTRICLY CHARGED." Anyone who so much as touched the locks, apparently, would be zapped. Inside, where I peered through the glass split and mended with duct tape, I could see mounds of tools, paintings, furniture, and dust—nothing that wasn't cracked, broken, yet so fiercely guarded. Then, I saw this letter taped to the glass from the inside:

> *The passing of a loving and dear friend. Now I'm not married so its not my wife But mans best freind "His Dog." My dog Bandito part husky disappeared from my home in Bucoda Friday Jan 3rd 1985. A neighbor reported that he heard a gun shot which woke him up 4 PM Saturday morning I hope you Bandito didn't die of a gun shot wound. I hear you were taken by force that you leave a house of good master a nice and loving. Im beginning to miss your presence at foot of my bed when I eat a meal your beging for a share that Im having Im glad that I had a part of your life you will be missed.*
>
>

*signed a old man of
Bucoda Wash
Mr. Nu*

Someday, to write an essay called "Looking for Mr. Nu," I will go back to Bucoda and find the man. My notebook reminds me I have this assignment. Mr. Nu lost Bandito. I can't afford to lose Mr. Nu.

GRAFFITI AND SHORT PHRASES

We are surrounded by bits of wisdom and humor, puns, proverbs, jingles, little prayers, short phrases that go suddenly deep in the midst of the passing flow. A writer takes them seriously by taking them down. It is important for me to know that someone at my college has written on the wall of a restroom stall, "How do you define success in college? Being as intelligent when you get out as when you started." It is important for me to write down my four-year-old daughter's assessment: "Papa, we have a cuckoo clock instead of a television, right?" I need to consider the implications of the warning at Bert Grim's Old Town Tattoo Parlor: "You must be 18 or older to be tattooed." I ponder the question on the marquee at the cleaners: "If your life were on VCR, would you watch it?"

What does it mean about American culture that a shirt at Nantucket proclaims, "He who dies with the most toys wins," while an Idaho bumper sticker holds, "My wife yes, my dog, maybe, my gun never"? I live with these short texts of American literature, give them a second chance to work on my mind by copying them small in my notebook. The hand-painted sign by a house in a poor neighborhood could launch a short story: "This is our home please dump your garbage elsewhere!" The words etched in the rearview mirror of a rental car could tease me into an essay about time and change: "Objects in mirror are closer than they appear."

Such passages might not actually appear in stories, poems, or essays I come to write. They lie behind the solitary work of the imagination, inviting it forward. In my daily writing life, such phrases work like known catalysts to bring the unknown story into being.

These language gifts surround me. While others seem to over-hear these gifts on occasion and by chance, I try to make the hearing and recording of them my central mission as a writer, and a key invitation to writing students. We start by taking dictation on the world, and then work together on what comes. The habit of listening attentively to quickly passing moments of coherence in the talk around us seems to train the mind to catch its own moments of discovery. Dreams get away if we don't tell them, or write them down. Thoughts do the same. The writer's greatest tool may be faith in a fragment. I try to train my mind to know that this thing I have overheard may be a moment's pleasure—*and* my invitation for a week's work. It is small, but it is mine. I heard it for a reason. No one else knows the story it is trying to tell.

In this way, the writing teacher is simply the one most con-sistently savoring the abundant pleasures of the common lan-guage. My students and I start each class by sharing recent discoveries from our notebooks, then we ask each other, "What might you do with that?" The best teaching happens by direct example—reading the world, showing delight in what we find, and inviting more.

I say to my students, "That moves. When will I get to read what you will write from this fine thing you have found?"

3

An Education in Presence:
When Literature Comes
to Life in
Student Journals

NEAL TOLCHIN

Neal Tolchin is associate professor of American literature at Hunter College and The Graduate School—CUNY. He specializes in 19th century and multi-cultural American literature. He is the author of Mourning, Gender, and Creativity in the Art of Herman Melville *(Yale UP, 1988). His current project is* Cultural Loss and Empowerment in American Literature.

Fay sat in a chair alongside my desk and waited. She stared off into space, clearly in pain. "Is there something you'd like to talk to me about," I hesitantly offered, as I tried to imagine the trouble this gentle, young student found herself in. Could she be pregnant? Had she failed an important exam? Silence. I suggested that we arrange for her to meet with someone in the personal counseling office. She looked at me fearfully. No, I thought, the codes of privacy and discretion of her Chinese background made counseling too frightening. More silence. I knew she couldn't talk about her problem to me at this point and yet her presence in my office was clearly a cry for help. As her professor last semester in "Literary Analysis and Argumentation," a small class of twenty or so students at a state university in which class sizes were usually in the hundreds, I might well be the only teacher that she had come to know. "Fay," I suggested, "I'll be in my office tomorrow. If you feel you can talk then come back."

When she returned the next day, I learned that Fay was indeed in trouble. And I apparently was its source. The previous semester we had read E. L. Doctorow's "A Writer in the Family." My students were keeping a reading journal, in which I was encouraging them to describe their response to what we read. I wanted them not to censor this response by filtering it through the conventions of what can and cannot be said in traditional academic discourse about literature. Instead, I encouraged them to write in their journals what they really felt and thought about in response to our readings, no matter how seemingly irrelevant. My theory was that as students responded to themes in the literature, they would also become aware of similar issues in their own lives. Their experiences would help to provide insights into the text, which would in turn cast sidelights on their lives, giving them a fresh perspective on common material. In Fay's case, as I was to learn, this technique had worked all too well.

Doctorow's story is about a young man whose father has recently died. An aunt asks him to write letters in his father's voice to his grandmother, who is being led to believe her son has not died. For Fay this was not merely a cute or contrived situation; she had been in the identical situation after her own father's death. Doctorow's situation dramatizes how the son's impersonation of his father's voice enables him to resolve his grief for his father by understanding that although his father seemed to be a conformist loser, he had never lost touch with the dreams of his youth. Fay's journal entry had been particularly illuminating about the psychological work Doctorow's protagonist was performing. Her writing had been wooden and lifeless up to this point, and when she read her journal to the class, she radiated pride. She understood it was a breakthrough piece of work. By the end of the semester, Fay was an enthusiastic English major, but the work of illumination begun by Doctorow's story was not yet complete for her.

Memories of her father, revived by writing about Doctorow, came vividly back to life for Fay. She began to remember things that she had long ago blocked out: her father had sexually molested her. As the pain of these buried feelings surfaced the following semester, Fay could no longer do her school work. It made sense then that she had sought me out for help. Wasn't I, after all, in some way responsible for the emotional paralysis she now felt? Hadn't I assigned the story about blocked grief and encouraged her to deeply respond to it?

By the end of the next semester, Fay once more was seated alongside my desk. A friend had put her in touch with a center for sexually abused children, and therapy had enabled her to finish the semester. The once quiet and somewhat passive young woman now spoke with tentative but growing firmness and energy about her plans for the future. Fay's transformation validated my feeling that teaching literature can be more than training students to be clever close readers. Her ordeal confirmed what I had learned from my own experience as a writer: to study literature was an adventure in self-exploration.

Doctorow's story put Fay in touch with blocked feelings about her father. Psychologically speaking, we could say that Fay "projected" her problems onto the protagonist. However, projection in this case is not simply the act of imputing one's emotional problems to the author. Rather, it is formed in response to, in dialogue with, conflicts we share with an author. Fay understood both the character and herself better as a result. Her self-analysis enabled her to incisively analyze Doctorow's insightful presentation of his character's conflicts with his father, which then deepened her understanding of her feelings toward her father. More importantly, Fay's skillful close reading of her response to Doctorow was a text she valued, one in which she was deeply invested because it was an act of self-discovery.

While revising my Ph.D. dissertation, I, like Fay, had experienced the transformative power of projection.[1] Although I had completed a lengthy draft of the dissertation, I had an undefined feeling of dissatisfaction that I had not gotten to the bottom of my topic—Melville and gender. When I stumbled across John Bowlby's *Loss*, an overview of research on mourning, and learned about delayed grief (i.e., mourning that we do not resolve, which goes underground in our psyches and can resurface decades later), I suddenly saw my topic in a deeper, more revealing light.

[1]My revised dissertation has been published as *Mourning, Gender, and Creativity in the Art of Herman Melville* (New Haven: Yale UP, 1988).

I began to see that the strange distortion of gender roles in Melville's work bore on the Victorian American cultural codes that assigned women the role of symbolizing restrained grief. I also learned that when a parent dies, the child is powerfully influenced by the surviving parent's grief. This opened my eyes to the influence on Melville of his relationship with his domineering mother. But it was only when I was well into my revision of the dissertation that I realized my interest in mourning and delayed grief was rooted in the personal, not just the literary.

When I was about Melville's age at the time he lost his father (twelve), my aunt died of complications following a heart operation my mother had encouraged her to have. Feeling responsible for her sister's death, my mother suffered a nervous breakdown. I vividly recalled witnessing the intensity of my mother's conflicted grief: her self-castigations were scary to me, especially as her personality had always seemed to me so forceful and self-assured. In years after, my mother suffered periodic bouts of depression, in which she re-experienced her unresolved grief. And when my father would enlist the aid of my brothers and myself in comforting my mother, we witnessed her speaking in a little girl voice of helplessness—a confusing and terrifying transformation.

What my research into mourning research helped me to see was that the difficulties my mother had in coming to terms with her sister's death deeply colored my own bereavement for my beloved aunt. This gave me a model for how Melville could have confused the conflicts of his own bereavement for his father with those of his mother's grief. I recalled a moment in my sixth-grade class when, without sensing the onset of powerful feelings, I suddenly began weeping. I was stunned by this because it came over me so suddenly and I believe it was the only time I expressed my feelings in this way about my aunt (I was not taken to the funeral). This displaced quality of grief, I began to realize, could play a key role in Melville's creativity. At moments when his fiction retriggered issues related to the loss of his father, the conflicts of his grief could emerge in his novels.

Now that I had become aware of what had empowered my interest in the role of blocked mourning in Melville, I knew that I must squarely face the role of projection in my work. Had I unconsciously transferred to Melville my own identity themes (to borrow Norman Holland's terminology)? Was this unresolved psychological issue in my own life helping me to identify evidence in Melville's life and art that bespoke similar issues in his life? Could projection be a heuristic device that plays a crucial role in supposedly disinterested scholarly research?

My experience of my mother's intense grief, I now believe, prepared me to empathize with the twelve-year-old Melville, experiencing his father's month-long deathbed mania and then his mother's intense bereavement, complicated by her anger at being abandoned by him to financial straits caused by his bankruptcy. As I reread *Moby-Dick* from this perspective, I began to understand how Ahab's mania and nobility were rooted in the conflicting images of his father that Melville's mother had bequeathed him. According to her Calvinist creed, deathbed mania was a sign of damnation. Yet her genteel upbringing also caused her to idealize her dead husband. My work on Melville taught me that the research project with which I was fascinated had derived from unresolved issues in my life, and that as I became self-conscious about this I empowered my work dialectically. My identity theme sharpened the focus on my research problems, and what I was learning about Melville's unresolved grief helped me to understand my own response to loss.

To show my students the power of projection as a way to respond to literature, I have come increasingly to emphasize the reading journal in my teaching of literature. Students often don't realize when their responses to the text offer insights the class finds valuable. By having them record their immediate and intimate response to literature, I teach them to value what our readings have stirred up within them. In my initial instructions about how to write their journal entries, I encourage them to continually link the underlying issues in literature to those in their own lives. I don't require that they do this. Yet many of the students who are initially resistant to this mode of writing are quite drawn to it by semester's end. Ideally, the journal will be a close reading both of the text and of the student's response to it. Or as one student described her journal, "It is a record of the connections I made with the literature of the period to the world of the present as filtered through my life." When they have reached this point, they are in a position to use their personal experiences to illuminate these issues in the literature and then to allow the literature to cast new light on their experiences.

I do not invent clever assignments to trick the student into using the journal to make connections between the literature and their life. I have found that most of my students are already making these links but censoring them out of their writing because they have been conditioned by previous English classes not to write about how they are really responding to what they read. Instead, they have been primed to switch into an English-class writing voice: to dutifully discuss images, general themes, in short, to be New Critics, or to talk about language in ways they know their English teachers will reward with high grades. I give them permission to write what they actually think and feel about what we read. My objective is not to turn them into writers of MLA articles but to encourage them to write with clarity and honesty about their response. They can voice freely their boredom, anger, confusion, and hopefully their excitement and enthusiasm as well. But I encourage them to explore these initial responses and analyze what in the literature and in their lives has led them to respond in this way. Not all journal entries are successful; some are dead ends. But others are written with the kind of energy and feeling one rarely experiences in conventional student essays.

At the outset of the semester I try to counteract what, traditionally, many writing teachers have inculcated in the student: edit yourself out of your writing. As one of my students wrote in her journal:

> *The first hurdle to get over before I even began the journal was reconditioning myself to believe that it was okay to say 'I believe' rather than 'one may believe.' Every since Mrs. Armstrong's eleventh grade English class in which she constantly x'd out all 'I's' in papers with a huge red pen, I have never written in the first person for a class.*

This student wrote that when she first learned about the requirement of keeping a journal, "my first thought was 'Oh, No!' I thought 'please, please just give a couple of tests and papers' ... The thought of having to respond to a book from inside myself rather than based on lectures, research and study horrified me. I am very good at observing how others feel and act but when it comes to myself I have great difficulty figuring out how I feel."

In responding to the first few journal entries, I try to give feedback on where the student can go further in exploring their response, and I ask that they respond to my suggestions in a revised entry. To create a supportive atmosphere, I emphasize positive elements in their journals. During the rest of the semester, I agree to read any entries the student is particularly enthused about (and some of the students need responses to all their entries), but I put the emphasis on sharing their journals in small-group work. I will also periodically ask that entries be handed in. Students can delete material they feel uncomfortable sharing in groups (or with me), although as the semester unfolds and students begin to trust each other, this occurs less frequently.

A crucial element in creating the kind of classroom atmosphere in which the students feel comfortable sharing their journals is to define my role not as the authority on the text but rather as member of a community of readers. In this sense, I serve as a role model for the students. I want them to feel that their response to what we read is as valid as mine, or any member of our reading community. I stress *community* to set the tone for our class as a group of people with equal privileges and with responsibilities to take care of each other. This becomes particularly important when one is sharing intimate responses. In sharing journal entries, my students have been remarkably supportive and encouraging of one another.

As a final paper, I ask the students to read their own journal and respond to it as a literary text.[2] Are there recurrent themes in the journal? What surprises them about what they've written? If the journal just seems chaotic, I ask that they describe the chaos, which usually leads to the discovery that there are topics to which they often return in their writing. I ask that they use this final paper as a chance to extend and deepen, to further reflect on, what are in fact their identity themes: the recurrent topics. This often is an exciting piece of writing for the student. As one wrote, "I was amazed at how much I disclosed about my personal life and how interesting some of my life experiences were. I found it a liberating experience."

By reading their journal as a literary text, their sense of writerly authority is validated. Invariably, they register a sense of pride, of feeling good about their writing. As one student reflected,

---

[2]This assignment, along with much of the tenor of my approach to teaching writing, has been inspired by Nancy Sommers's graduate course "Theories of Composition."

As I reread my entries, I found it odd that I could actually respond on paper as me. The best aspect of my journal is that it is mine. These writings are what I believe about the books and how they made and will continue to make me feel. In the future, I will be able to reread these entries and the personal associations will trigger thoughts and memories about the characters in the books as well as my life.

For this student, her journal is a valued text, one to which she has already returned and which she looks forward to re-reading in the future because she has really learned something about herself there.

As a reader of student journals, I too value them for the energy and excitement the students invest in them. Many are simply so much better written, and more fun to read, than the standard term paper or essay style exam. Through the journals I also get to know my students better and they get to know each other more intimately. This is particularly valuable for the quiet students, and I am often grateful to the journals for giving me a better basis on which to evaluate the participation of those students who simply are not comfortable sharing in class. The journals, invaluably, prime the students for class discussion. Often, when we are not sharing journals but engaging in free-wheeling discussion of a text, I observe students glancing into their journals to refresh their memories about their response. Sometimes they simply demand that we listen to what they said in their journals.

The journal teaches the student the value of substantive revision. When they add onto an entry after class discussion, they reassess their earlier response. In the final essay, they distill, refine, and reflect on their earlier ideas. As one student realized, "I think my journal is sometimes untrue to what I feel in general about a work. These writings are solely my 'first impressions'. . . . Now, a month later, I remember the book much more positively than I seem to feel in the journal."

In a class on cultural identity in American literature, a student's sense of frustration at knowing little about her mixed ethnic heritages had caused her early in the semester to disclaim interest in "bloodspirits and ancestor stories." In her final essay she realized, "I didn't want to deal with these questions, because I felt that the conflict created through the mutually hostile cultures I grew up in would touch upon too many memories that would in turn bring back frustration and disillusionment." But the readings, particularly Toni Morrison's *Beloved,* had taught her that

> *if the negative memory is retrieved, the anger loses its power. If I analyze my roots, I might be angry at the injustices of the moral systems of my cultures. By defining these injustices more clearly I can start dealing with them.*
>
> *I find now that roots can not be denied, even if we choose not to give them much significance they affect us through our parents, ancestors and collective history. I still can't see myself emerging in my search for my ethnic identity. But I do see myself reconfronting this history, to maybe find out its function and meaning in my identity.*

By realizing that "our past is also carried by others," she had come up with a plan for reclaiming her cultural identity: "if we find these people they can act as keys to unlock our memories lying dormant."

The most gratifying part of working with journals for me as a teacher is to witness how much the students learn about themselves through their journals and how this deepens their insights into and love for literature. In evaluating the journals, what distinguishes the most accomplished ones is the students' ability to relate the literature to their lives and then to bring these insights about themselves back to the text. After reading Barbara Myerhoff's *Number Our Days,* "something magical happened" for one of my students.

> *I began to hear the voice of my belated and beloved Italian grandfather, who was associated with a senior citizens' center much like the one in the book. I remembered the wonderful times I spent with him there . . . The connection became powerful, and I could almost feel the presence of my grandfather as I wrote this passage. I felt so sad for the people who felt isolated from their children because their cultures were so different. I do not regret for one minute taking the opportunity to celebrate my proudly Italian grandfather. In a way, this is what Myerhoff does: she celebrates the lives of these marvelous people, who are proud of their Jewish heritage. So, in a sense, she influenced me to do just that, and I'm glad I did it!*

By linking the literature to her life, this student gains insight into how Myerhoff constructs her ethnic identity through the celebration of the senior citizens.

In a powerful moment in his final essay, an African–American student described his response to Frederick Douglass's *Narrative of the Life of a Slave:*

> *I realized, reading this book, what feelings could arise from living under slavery. I've never felt what true oppression is like, but I've also never had a book to grip my insides and leave me unable to speak, and so moved by anger that hours after reading, I couldn't stop tears from streaming down my face.*

In his first journal entry, this student had written about a lack of knowledge of his ethnic background and of not really having a cultural identity.

> *Many times after re-reading the journal entry for this book and the first journal entry, I would feel a combination of anger and shame. Anger, for not having had the opportunity to receive this knowledge earlier, and shame for my lack of it altogether.*

For me, this student's anger and shame vividly illuminate the emotive reality of Douglass's text. When he shared this entry with the class, the pain Douglass evoked in him opened up the text for the class and freed up other African–American students in the class to discuss how it felt to be exposed to their heritage through Douglass's unflinching portrayal of it. Yet this student's response also initiated a fascinating discussion of the absence of an open expression of anger and shame in Douglass's text. Our personal responses to the text led into a discussion of the formal issues of the representation of emotion in slave narratives.

I learn much from my students' journals, as I witness their discovery of who they are and what they value. This education in presence has caused me to reevaluate my goals as a teacher. Knowing how powerfully literature can influence my students' lives, I construct courses and choose texts that will speak to the issues that dominate their lives. When putting together a syllabus I think about the incredibly diverse backgrounds of my Hunter College students. In the furor over opening up the canon at Stanford University, discussions often fail to mention that minority groups are now the majority of Stanford students and that these students played a key role in demanding that Stanford's curriculum reflect the realities of their lives and backgrounds. As a teacher, I no longer see myself as an imparter of information, but rather as a participant in the unfolding of my students' lives. I want their journal to be a place of growth for them. And I hope to share with them the excitement of discovering how powerfully a work of literature can speak to our lives.

4

Teaching What We Know About Revision

MIMI SCHWARTZ

Mimi Schwartz likes writing, teaching, and the connections be-
tween the two. Her book, **Writing for Many Roles,** *and software*
program **Prewrite** *began in courses she teaches at Stockton State*
College, where she is an associate professor of writing. Her current
interests in autobiography, revision, and the personal essay are
reflected in articles in **College English, College Composition and**
Communication, *and* **English Journal,** *among others, as well as*
in **Writer's Craft, Teacher's Art.** *She is currently working on a*
creative nonfiction book, **Swimming above the Black Line.**

In the foreword to *On Becoming a Novelist,* Raymond Carver says
of his former teacher John Gardner:

> *He believed in revision, endless revision; it was something close to*
> *his heart and something he felt vital for writers at every stage of*
> *development.*

I identify with that. I, too, practice endless revision—ten, twenty,
thirty drafts for most essays or fiction; two or three drafts, at
least, for memos, reports, and letters worth their salt. And revision is the foundation of my teaching as well. On the first day
of class I tell my students, "I teach rewriting, not writing," and

explain how my whole course is designed to encourage revision strategies and skill. Like John Gardner, my own experience as a writer has convinced me that success depends on this process, which I, too, see as vital "for writers at every stage of development." Consequently, whatever I'm teaching—whether it's basic writing, autobiography, or advanced composition—my pedagogy focuses on revision as the key for turning chaos into ordered thought, vague notions into polished texts.

In concrete terms, this means that a student portfolio in my class includes not only clean copy but "finished" work that looks like this—especially if a student has no word processor:

> ....Playing football here is a unique experience. You
> should have seen ~~the shocked expressions of the~~ what happened at the pep rally
> ~~students~~ when the coach introduced me ~~as a member of~~ as one of the new
> quarterbacks
> ~~the team during a pep rally.~~ At first, no one clapped
> or cheered when my name was called. not even my teammates. You could have
> heard a pin drop. ~~But the coach kept repeating, "Come on,~~ With repeated encouragement from the
> Give him a big hand." and
> ~~coach~~ they finally applauded ~~with staggered~~ Should I put this portion
> hesitation.... back. I don't miss it!

(Handwritten marginal notes: "what did the coach do?"; "what were position players?";)

Even with word processors, I insist on drafts with this kind of revision history—representing interactions between writer, readers, and text—before a clean copy is printed out. "What on earth for?" you may be saying, particularly if, like Frank D'Angelo, you are more of a Mozart planner than a Beethoven discoverer,[1] or, using Muriel Harris's terms,[2] you are more of a one drafter than a multi-drafter like me.

I encourage such drafts because they provide students with a window into their own revision process, giving a visual record of their decision making: where and how they've improved on earlier drafts, where they have not. Even more important, how-

[1]From "The Art of Composing," *Writers on Writing*, vol. II, ed. Tom Waldrep (New York: Random House, 1988).
[2]"Composing Behaviors of One- and Multi-Draft Writers," *College English* (February 1989).

ever, are the revision values that this messiness conveys: that revision is a creative act and therefore chaotic; that the writer must keep control of this act (readers suggest options, but make no changes); and that the ideal text is out there waiting to be found, and life is exhilarating when you do. But don't count on such finds every time, I also warn, or you won't risk much, and it's the risk taking, plus revising strategies and skill, that eventually lead writers to their best writing. That's what I've found as a writer (I'm now on draft eight of this essay)—and that's what I want to convey to my students.

Obviously, not everyone shares my fervor for revision—either as writers or as teachers. Although most of us incorporate some revision into our courses, many find other aspects of the composing process—rhetorical structures, audience awareness, grammar—more central to writing pedagogy. And with good success! In my department, for example, there is great variety, even among our best teachers, as to the value and methods of teaching revision. Over the years, I have often wondered how others teach well without stressing revision, since I can't. What do they do instead, I've asked myself, and how are their approaches connected to their own composing processes?

This year, thanks to two agreeable colleagues who are also outstanding writing teachers, I was able to find out. They agreed to take part in a two-stage interview that would enable me to identify (1) their strategies as revisers, and (2) their revision pedagogy as teachers. To provide a concrete basis for the interviews, they supplied samples of their own writing, including drafts, as well as syllabi from several different courses. They also filled out Revision Profile Forms, which I've used successfully to define revision patterns in other revision research.[3]

What I found in this informal study is that how we revise definitely shapes how we teach revision. Two of us, both extensive multi-draft revisers, make revision an essential element in assignments—but not in the same way. Our third colleague, generally a one-drafter who "almost never revises on paper," as she puts it, doesn't give multi-draft assignments at all. Instead, she emphasizes internal revising techniques that work for her. All of us succeed, I think, because what we preach and practice in revision are closely connected. Unlike the teacher/writers in

[3]See my article "Revision Profiles," *College English* (December 1983).

Marie Nelson's research,[4] who ignored their own processes when teaching students—and consequently disliked the teaching of writing—we all try to pass on our successful strategies. Let me define these teacher-writer connections in more detail to show how revision attitudes, goals, and strategies affect our respective classrooms.

TEACHER #1: MIMI SCHWARTZ:
FINDING MY VOICE AND SOME NUGGETS

In looking over my drafts—both fiction and nonfiction—I realize there are two revision goals that shape my writing and my teaching. Both involve searches: the first is to find the right voice; the second, to borrow from James Dickey, is to find the nuggets in fifty tons of dirt. Finding the voice comes first. It determines who I am in the text, what my relationship is with the material and the audience. If I like the person I hear, I can move quickly; but if the voice sounds stiff, or whiny, or cutesy, I can be stuck on that page for awhile. My goal, as one friend put it, "is to write something that sounds effortlessly natural, like a perfect first draft." That usually takes a long time and lots of paper.

Hearing helps me to re-see the text, and vice versa. Like Eudora Welty in *One Writer's Beginning*, "When I write and the sound of it comes back to my ears, then I act to make my changes. ... The sound of what falls on the page begins the process of testing it for truth for me. . . . "[5] Listening to my voice makes me see the world with more perspective: if I sound strident, or cranky, or undeservedly flip, I temper the voice and with it the arguments that go with it. In an op-ed editorial I did for the *New York Times* called "Who's Stealing the Silver?" I wrote initially in fury—our insurance company had refused to pay for our stolen silver—and had it promptly rejected. Several months later, I came across it, realized how peevish I sounded, and rewrote it with more detachment, a bemused E. B. White kind of frustration. It was a much better piece—and they took it.

A similar struggle for voice took place in writing this paper. I wanted to write up "research"—but with a personal, not disem-

---

[4]"Bridging the Paradigm Gap—Adopting an Expert-Practitioner Stance," *English Record* XXXIV (1983).
[5]Harvard UP, 1983, 12.

bodied voice. Yet, if I were too personal, would people believe my findings? The conflict came to a head early on—when I wrote on page 2:

> *"What on earth for?" I can hear you muttering, particularly if, like many of my colleagues, you don't revise much.*

I suddenly felt too combative as if only I knew what's right. I imagined my readers saying with irritation: "That may be your experience, but it's not mine," so I kept rewriting until, a half-hour later, I had:

> *"What on earth for?" I can hear many of you wondering, particularly if, like Frank D'Angelo, you are more of a Mozart planner than a Beethoven discover, or, using Muriel Harris' terms, you are more of a one drafter than a multi-drafter—like me.*

Invoking D'Angelo and Harris made me feel part of a larger tradition. Switching to "wondering" and adding "like me" made me feel friendlier—while still acknowledging our potential differences on revision. That was the voice I wanted. Once I resolved its tension without feeling compromised, I proceeded with more confidence; the paper would work after all.

Voice, to me, emerges out of the struggle to find an authentic self that is true to the material and effective to the audience. Revision is the means to resolve this struggle, which is why I switched back to "muttering" and finally to "I can imagine you saying" on the last draft. "Wondering" felt too homogenized somehow, as if I were giving up some sense of self.

Revising for voice is central to my revision pedagogy as well. I want my students to become attuned to voice and revise until *they* like what *they* hear. I point out stiffness and ask them to rewrite the lines more naturally. I encourage in-class readarounds of early drafts, so students can hear what they sound like and what others sound like—and revise accordingly. I want them to feel comfortable as central characters in their public texts (as they are in their journals), not anonymous voices offstage. Otherwise, they are not self-invested, and I don't think they will write well.

If I hear no authentic voice—as in one draft which began: "Looking for influential experiences could most easily be summed up in a barrage of passing instances of existence"—I say, "Rewrite from scratch. Start again." But once there is a convincing voice, I shift to my second revision strategy: finding the nuggets in fifty tons of dirt. This involves sifting through irrelevancies for the power of the text—its rhythms, key imagery, ideas, and form. Whether it be my text or someone else's, I ask the same questions, trying to mine the draft for buried clues: Where do I need more? What's the shape of this piece? What's this draft really about? And I follow hunches, especially when I'm the writer, to find the answers. That's why revision, for me, is a creative act, fueled more by intuition than by reason.

Making the *right* changes, however, depends not only on reading the draft well but on understanding one's revision patterns. For example, in nonfiction, I tend to be an underwriter on early drafts and have learned to re-read with the idea: Where must I open it up? In fiction and autobiography, however, I usually overwrite initially, trying to get everything of even remote interest out on the page. Then I cut back, asking myself: What's frivolous and what's essential? until I know what the piece is about.

I want my students to learn how to read *their* drafts based on *their* revision profiles. Developing that skill is more important to me than helping them perfect their texts. That's why I value "messy" experiments and risk taking that fails—even on final drafts—more than I do neat, but unmemorable texts. My comments act as initial prompts for students to follow. If I ask a lot of questions, they must expand their texts in revision. If I bracket a lot (which means "consider cutting") they must try to tighten their prose. Two or three papers into the semester, we review their portfolio with its revision history, and they begin to understand what revision strategies *they* need to develop. If, by the end of the course, my students have learned how to re-read drafts with an eye for nuggets and an ear for voice, it's been a good semester.

TEACHER #2: G.T. LENARD:
LOOKING FOR AN ORGANIZED STRUCTURE

My colleague G.T. Lenard does not revise unless she has to—as when she had to satisfy her dissertation committee. "I probably cut more text than ever in my life," she says of that encounter. But when left to her own devices, she rarely revises. A $1,000 prize-winning essay on smoking, which she wrote last summer, published in the *Phillip Morris* Magazine, was completed in one two-hour sitting. Her syllabi and writing assignments, all highly structured and detailed, are usually done in one twelve-hour sitting. She carries the ideas around with her for months before she sits down, however.

G.T.'s revision attitudes come from her schooling, she says. She went to Catholic grammar school where cross-outs were not permitted and there were no "do-overs" on assignments. "We had a boat load of writing, but never did things over for a grade, only as a punishment. The nuns did read everything and got it back the next day with stars and angels. I liked that."

As a result, G.T. revises in her head, using talk (she calls it "freewriting of the mouth") rather than written words to reformulate her ideas. "It's a good thing I live alone," she says. She sounds out ideas out loud—in the car or pacing through the house—for days before she starts writing, and on longer projects such as a journal article, she treats a friend who is a good listener to dinner. "I'll pay and you don't have to say a thing. Just nod once in a while," G.T. assures her. So for G.T., as for me, voice is important—but it shapes her texts *before* rather than after she has something on the page.

However, her primary focus is on structure, a way to organize the material. Once she has that and an opening line, which she will keep rewriting on a fresh piece of paper until she has one that works, she is on her way. She does have some cross-outs now, and some inserts, but her drafts are immaculate compared to mine.

In the classroom, G.T. teaches what has worked for her: brainstorming out loud for a topic, an angle, and a structure. Before an assignment, she spends half a class discussing ways to organize the paper. She also gives many assignments that she gives back the next class, graded, like the nuns did in her old grade school days, and with response. But instead of stars and angels, she writes "copious comments," she says, both in margins and endnotes. "I want them to see me as an active, interested reader. If they work hard, I will too." Hence, the quick turnaround.

Michael—There is a great deal of charm in your style, but—alas!—it's too often "hidden" by those errors. Your spelling—!! Goodness! Keep a list of your misspellings, ok? That way, at least you won't keep spelling the same words wrong!

Thomas—You raise some strong points here, and I'm pleased with the material you selected. I think your organization started falling apart near the end, though. Why the short paragraphs, etc.? Getting tired? The problem areas are indicated within the text. Watch "hanging quotes" etc.

G.T.'s comments, although critical, are friendly rather than harsh in tone. She comes across as optimistic—that they *can* do better next time—and evidently they believe her, judging from the lively office hours she holds. Students are always waiting to get her help, but not with sullen faces.

G.T.'s revision pedagogy is based on a carry-over philosophy, also from her grade school days: that students will "revise," based on her comments—but on the next paper. She gives fifteen to twenty short papers a term, so they have plenty of chances to succeed. And they do, judging from the performance of her students, many of them basic writers, who do well on our school-wide writing test.

TEACHER #3: JACK CONNOR: BUILDING A NEST OUT OF FRAGMENTS

When he's not directing our college's writing program, Jack Connor is a successful nonfiction writer who gets up to write from 5:30 to 8 or 9 each morning, particularly about his specialty: birds and bird-watching. His book, *The Complete Birder,* is a 1988 Book of the Month Club alternate selection, and he is currently working on his second book, *A Season at the Point,* about the hawks and hawk watchers at Cape May Point, New Jersey.

Like me, Jack is a multi-drafter who depends on revision to improve his texts, and we share many common attitudes towards revision: that it is a creative rather than error-correcting act, that it is messy, chaotic, recursive, exhilarating, and hard work. "Clean rough drafts are the sign of a lazy writer," he tells his students on the first day of class, and he reinforces this belief with a handout of assumptions, which include:

- *(#3) Writing is like walking a labyrinth; you can't go straight.*
- *(#4) The more writing the better.*
- *(#6) The more revisions the better.*
- *(#10) We get what we slave for.*

Like Peter Elbow, Don Murray, Richard Marius, and Ann Ber-
thoff, to name just a few, Jack is in the rewrite-for-discovery
tradition of composing.

Jack's metaphor for his writing process is that of nest building:
"I work like a bird, building a nest—a fragment from here and
there, woven together, moved around, until a new fragment
appears and is added on." After reviewing his drafts for an
article, "Owling," that he wrote recently for *Harrowsmith* magazine, I find his analogy a very fitting one. As you can see in this
excerpt from draft 1, he begins with bits and pieces of phrasing,
many privately abbreviated, such as "abt" for "about," "ty" for
"they are," which accrete on the page.

Order, connections, relevancy, all come several drafts later as
isolated images of content begin to take shape into larger units
of ideas—sentences, even paragraphs, some of which he will use,
some of which he'll save for later—for other stories. "Every story
has a 'Frag File' on my computer," he tells me, "where I store
all the material that I might use. So if I have to cut because of
space or audience or focus, I do it more easily; its time may come
sometime later."

Unlike G.T. and me, Jack is not concerned with voice initially—
just in getting ideas out of his head and onto the page. Gathering
and then shaping content are his first revision goals. Once he
has these, then voice becomes important, particularly in finding
a good lead. "Owling" underwent many changes in lead and
voice—but after draft 9!

"The first thing to know about owls is they're out there. Numbers saw whet. . . . " (#1)

"The first thing to know about owls is they are far more common than most people realize, probably more common and widespread than anyone knows. . . . " (#9)

"How well do you know the birds of your neighborhood? Can you name the only bird from your neighborhood, the most widespread bird in the Western Hemisphere? . . . " (#13)

"The best guide I know to owling as it should be done is a children's book: Owl Moon *by Jane Yolen and John Schoenherr. A father wakes his little daughter late one mid-winter night; they bundle up and walk through snow to the woods. It's the girl's first night of owling, but she knows she should not say a word. . . . " (final)*

This article gave him more trouble than usual because of two external constraints: (1) How was he going to tell an audience of non-birders about owl watching without sounding stuffy and pedantic? (2) How was he going to handle the use of tape recordings to lure owls when he was against the practice? In the end he solved both problems—but it took sixteen drafts.

This need to be true to self while still satisfying content and audience constraints (his editor had insisted on including information on using tapes) is what makes writing a challenge to committed writers. As Richard Marius says in his essay, "How I Write?": "The trick is to make someone want to read what you have to say and enjoy it and learn from it." Or, as Joan Didion puts it: to resolve the tensions of a piece is what real revision is all about. Students, too often, don't engage in this struggle. They write just to please the teacher, not themselves. So they don't revise much.

Jack's revision goals, like mine, are reflected in his revision pedagogy. Because an initial fluidity is essential to his own composing, he wants students to experience the same—and not lock themselves into a set form prematurely. Consequently, students write four or five discovery drafts, often with different topics and approaches. Only then do they choose one to develop into an essay, revising this several times, based on group and teacher response. It's a two-week process with lots of messy drafts.

One part of his revision process is not reflected in his pedagogy: the use of reader response to work in progress. He says he rarely shows his work to anyone before it's mostly finished, but he does require students to act as editors for each other throughout the process. "I have a strong sense of audience; they don't," Jack explains. "Peer group response, I hope, gives them some." However, Jack did show his wife draft 9 of "Owling," and it was she who mentioned the children's story, which gave him his final lead.

What can we say about revision from all this? Certainly not that there's one way to do it—or teach it. In fact, our diversity as teacher/revisers confirms the danger of adopting a uniform revision pedagogy, whether it be the think-outline-draft model or the freewrite–multi-draft model. Writers and teachers need more room to maneuver than that; that's what revision as a creative act is all about.

More important than prescriptive formulas is exposure to a variety of revision options,[6] taught by people who use them enthusiastically. If students, for example, had been taught by Jack, G.T., and me in their sixteen years in school, they'd know about voice, discovery drafts, structure, brainstorming with others, and how to read first drafts. Our diversity enriches them. We pass on what works best for us as successful practitioners—*that* is what is essential—and they, as David Huddle says elsewhere in this book, will "take what they need."

WORKS CITED

D'Angelo, Frank. "The Art of Composing." *Writers on Writing*. Vol. II. Ed. Tom Waldrep. New York: Random House, 1988.

Gardner, John. "Foreword." *On Becoming a Novelist*. New York: Harper, 1984.

Harris, Muriel. "Composing Behaviors of One- and Multi-Draft Writers." *College English* (February 1989).

Marius, Richard. "How I Write." *Writers on Writing*. Vol. II. Ed. Tom Waldrep. New York: Random House, 1988.

[6]We, as teacher/writers, can also benefit from this. After doing this study, I decided to set up a Jack "frag file" for this paper, and I tried talking through my ideas—out loud, G.T. style—as I drove home from school one day.

Nelson, Marie. "Bridging the Paradigm Gap—Adopting an Expert-Practitioner Stance." *English Record* XXXIV (1983).

Schwartz, Mimi. "Revision Profiles." *College English* (December 1983).

Welty, Eudora. *One Writer's Beginnings*. Cambridge, MA: Harvard UP, 1984.

5

Finding a Family, Finding a Voice: A Writing Teacher Teaches Writing Teachers

LYNN Z. BLOOM

Lynn Z. Bloom is a professor of English and holds the Aetna Chair of Writing at the University of Connecticut. She has written more than a dozen books, ranging from Doctor Spock: Biography of a Conservative Radical *to* The New Assertive Woman *to* Fact and Artifact: Writing Nonfiction. *Writing this essay was a turning point for her as writer and teacher: "having taken the risks that "Finding a Family" identifies, I'm committed to more and more daring writing, more creative, more personal, far more difficult— and also more fun—than any of the conventional academic writing I've done over the past thirty years." Fittingly, she is now working on a book on first-person writing called* Our Stories, Our Selves: Reading, Researching, Writing Autobiography.

A paradigm shift, says Thomas Kuhn, arises in response to a crisis. Old ways don't work, old explanations don't fit, and a crisis makes apparent the need for a new paradigm that fits better. This is the story of how three crises, two new, one of longstanding, converged to precipitate a paradigm shift in the way I teach writing teachers to teach writing. In the twinkling of an eye, the class metamorphosed from students in the process of learning about teaching in order to teach writing to students in the process of becoming writers in order to teach writing. Having effected the change, quite by accident, I can't go back; the new paradigm has supplanted the old.

I had taught "Teaching Composition," a graduate course in composition theory and pedagogy required of all new TAs, on and off for a decade, and I was looking forward to teaching it again at Virginia Commonwealth University. Following a widely accepted paradigm that was familiar, workable, and comfortable, I knew exactly what I would do. My students would read enough central works of rhetorical theory and composition research to enable them to sail, rather than stagger, through their first semester in the classroom. They would chart their course according to the principles and practices of such master mariners as Lindemann, Shaughnessy, Tate and Corbett, and Graves; their own teaching would mirror mine, which would of course model the best available information.

Initially the TAs would write an analysis of their own composing processes, to help them understand the process-oriented composition course they were teaching. They'd analyze a master's style. Later on, they would compile an annotated bibliography of current research and use these sources in a term paper of their choice. But whether or not these new teachers of writing wrote much or cared much about their own writing except to produce the requisite papers in appropriate academic form was beyond the expectations of myself or indeed of any of our graduate offerings other than writing workshops. Even though I write all the time (a day without writing is a day lost forever), I would not impose that additional burden on my students. They already had enough to do.

In my role as instructor I would provide an exemplary model of a professional writing teacher: always prepared, always able to anticipate their questions and answer them, always cheerfully in control. I could do no less. So I launched into the first day's ritual introduction to the course, but as I enthusiastically outlined what we'd do and why, it became apparent that something was wrong. The students seemed perplexed when I asked what writing assignments they were giving their freshmen. They looked unhappy when I suggested they bring in a sample of the diagnostic freshman essay to discuss in class, and finally, when I asked them to prepare a syllabus for the first two weeks of class, they admitted that only two of the fourteen somber students around the conference table were actually teaching. Some were tutoring in the writing center; some were grading papers for professors in literature courses; some had fellowships that freed them from other work; some were just taking the course for fun. Furthermore, the second edition of Lindemann's *A Rhetoric for Writing Teachers*, which I had intended as the core of the course, was delayed by the publisher; it wouldn't be available for a month, maybe longer. By the end of this very, very long ninety-minute session, I knew I would have to discard my well-wrought, carefully refined semester syllabus and redo the whole course.

In the two days between class sessions (we met twice a week) I began the walk along the tightrope that stretched from experience to innocence. Being by nature a risk taker (no, I don't ride Harley-Davidsons or dive off the fifteen-meter board), I am always trying new things—jobs, book ideas, and now, the riskiest of all, some creative nonfiction and poetry. (In the process of learning how to do it I am finally finding the welcome, personal voice I have for a lifetime been too scared to use—which balances the discomfort and vulnerability of public exposure.) So I moved headlong toward the innocent, the unknown end. In risk taking I would do risk teaching.

Because my students had no students of their own, I decided to ask them to examine their own writing. For a decade I had been asking students in virtually all my classes to write a first paper on "How I Write" as a way of helping themselves and me to better understand their composing process(es), and to anticipate and correct pitfalls. However, such papers, which I used to find fascinating, were becoming predictable to all of us; "How I Write" was the equivalent of "What I Did on My Summer Vacation" to these students, who had come of age in a process-oriented curriculum. Then, after all these years, I finally recognized the obvious—what good was a process without a compelling motive to use it? "Why I Write" had to precede "How I Write." And I knew that it would be far more difficult to write such a paper than "How I Write," but there was no alternative.

I began the next class, my once elegant and comprehensive syllabus, embodying the old paradigm, now reduced to a few tentative key words, by announcing the first writing assignment, "Why I Write." "Here I am," I said, "trying to model for you the Right Way to Give a Writing Assignment, and I'm doing it all wrong. I usually like to talk an assignment through with my students, focusing on useful key words" (major ideas, primary traits) "and appropriate rhetorical strategies, anticipating the problems, and offering suggestions for How to Do It. We look at some sample papers to see what other students have done."

"But I can't do these things with this assignment. I've never given it before" (How could I, in thirty years of teaching, have overlooked the obvious?) "so I don't know what to expect. I don't know why you write, but I do know that if writing is important to you your paper will be very revealing and it will be very hard to do. It's not fair," I continued, "to ask students who don't know the teacher and whom the teacher doesn't know to expose themselves on a personal level before the class has had time to create a community of trust and understanding, and yet I'm asking you to do this." (So much for the exemplary model.) "We can read why George Orwell and Joan Didion and Elie Wiesel say they write" (I distributed copies of their essays for the next session), "and we can see what the writers in *In Praise of What Persists* and *The Paris Review* series say, and we will—but maybe their reasons aren't your reasons. I tell you what" (I hesitated before taking the plunge because I knew the water would be cold and that I would be vulnerable, even, to drowning), "I'll go first, and we'll see what we can learn from my experience."

I had always been reluctant to impose my writing on my students. The focus of our classes should be properly on their work, not mine. I suspected I could write better than they could, and I didn't want to establish a climate of competition. (But this class contained a published poet and a prize-winning novelist, so the students could set the competence level for their peers.) Yet I could think of no other way to establish a climate for teaching writing as a process than by examining the question fundamental to that process—not "Why do it?" but "Why do *I* want to do it?"—and now I believe there is no other way.

"Teaching Composition" was getting tougher, unpredictable and therefore potentially out of control, though the students seemed very willing to explore "Why I Write," especially since I'd volunteered to test the waters. Our class, myself included, had also agreed to keep notebooks of reactions, not only to the

assigned and eclectic readings but to what went on in class; we'd
see what we could learn from the writing in progress and the
teaching in process.

The character of the course—an unstructured, off-balance,
ad-lib response to a crisis, like street theater in comparison with
a scripted play on a proscenium stage—was becoming a metaphor for my personal life. My husband, also a professor and
writer, and always cheerfully healthy, had begun waking up with
headaches. After waking earlier and earlier and sometimes not
sleeping at all, he consulted our usually cheerful dentist who
said, "Nope, it's not a toothache," and sent him off to our usually
cheerful internist, who suspected sinus problems and prescribed
ten days of decongestant. But the headaches got worse, and the
internist, no longer cheerful, sent my husband, who was having
difficulty reading by this time, to the local ENT specialist. Or-
dinarily a dramatic joker who treated even accident victims with
puns and funny faces, this doctor said, impassively, "I can see
something in there, but I can't tell what it is," and sent him to
a specialist at the state's major medical center, the Medical College of Virginia. By this time I was driving my husband everywhere he needed to go, for he could not see well enough to
drive, though with blind faith he continued to teach.

In class I felt like an Easter candy, with an eggshell veneer
over a liquid center; poke it and I'd collapse, the interior running
out. I was terrified that I would become a widow. At home, I
masked my tension in Girl Scout good cheer. After one long,
sleepless night I couldn't cry anymore and forced myself to eat
and to swim and to go to bed and even to play hostess to a
succession of houseguests, some from overseas, invited months
before. "We don't have anywhere else to go," they announced
from Dulles Airport, "you have to take us in." And so we did.

In this context I wrote "Why I Write." For the first time in
my literary life I could be uninhibited; graduate school training
had made me such a self-effacing writer that I'd never before
written anything except poetry in the first person. In relation to
the mortal combat being waged in our household, everything
else became a trivial pursuit. I was finally free to say what I
wanted; our existential crisis was, at least, liberating.

Only I wasn't free. At least, not on the first draft, or the second,
or the third. The first time through I wrote the easy part: "I
write because I can't not write. From the moment I learned to

read, enamored of the joys of Dr. Seuss, I knew I wanted to write. I thought at the age of six that to delight readers with words was the most wonderful thing in the world. I still think so." Only later did I have the courage to add, "To write is to touch one's readers, to make friends and risk enemies, to become a member of the human family—to belong, even in exile."

That first version was a piece of cake, six pages in two hours—a lot faster than I usually write, even with the computer. Maybe what I was asking my students to do wasn't so hard after all, though as I commented at the time in my teacher/writer notebook, "The metamorphosis from child reader to adult writer dashing off book after article after book makes the act of writing seem pretty simple, and pretty simple-minded, and unbelievable."

Indeed, the reasons for writing that we were discussing in class didn't make it sound that easy. George Orwell's "Why I Write" is a political manifesto: "My starting point is always a feeling of partisanship, a sense of injustice. . . . I write because there is some lie that I want to expose, some fact to which I want to draw attention" (394). Orwell's motive resonates in Joan Didion's claim, in another "Why I Write," that all serious writers say *"listen to me, see it my way, change your mind"* (17). The message of Holocaust survivor Elie Wiesel is unfailingly moral; in "Why I Write: Making No Become Yes," he explains that he writes as a witness to the memory of the Holocaust victims:

> *I owe them my roots and my memory. I am duty-bound to serve as their emissary, transmitting the history of their disappearance, even if it disturbs, even if it brings pain. Not to do so would be to betray them, and thus myself. . . . Why do I write? To wrench those victims from oblivion. To help the dead vanquish death. (24, 27)*

The day before my paper was due I started at 9 A.M. to polish it—an hour's task, I anticipated. By 4 P.M. I needed a break; at 9 P.M. I was still writing; I finally finished, drained, at 1 A.M. The resulting nine-page version wasn't much longer than the original draft, but the substance had changed considerably as I imposed a grid of the hard stuff over the original text. Why I write—as Orwell and Didion and Wiesel know full well—is who I am, and when I had plumbed "the deep heart's core" I knew I had said enough.

In elementary school, I told my students, I wrote to distance myself from conventional classmates—I wrote satires (about them) while they wrote yet again about their summer vacations; writing was social criticism. In high school I wrote to find a voice, to distance myself from my overbearing, "*paterfamilias* of four good German names (and a nickname of 'Odd')," who sought to impose his pompous, professorial style on my writing as on my life; writing was rebellion. In college I wrote to learn what I had to say and in graduate school and afterward I wrote to understand what others (writers, especially) had to say and how they said it. Writing was profession. So I wrote my way into job after job, too often filling others' demands for reports, reviews, encyclopedia articles, critical essays, textbooks, chapters of other people's books. In writing so much as somebody's professor, somebody's colleague, somebody's friend, I was losing my voice.

I was also writing, however, in hopes that my parents would be once again proud and "would invite me, the published author, back into the family they had thrown me out of, stunned, at twenty-four when I married out of their non-religion, a Jew." But "my father carefully misread my major books, the ones the reviewers especially liked, and ignored the rest. He never praised one syllable." I said all this in the essay for my students; I told them what I had never told anyone in public before, more even than my sister and brother knew. How could I make myself so vulnerable to the very students, whom I still didn't know very well, whose authority figure I was supposed to be? How could I live with them for the rest of the semester? But—I took a deep breath—how could I not write "Why I Write" without being as candid with them and tough with myself as I expected them to be in their own writing?

So I concluded the essay: My husband, "best critic and best friend," and the job security and independence that have come from doctoring and mastering academic writing have enabled me to regain my voice. I love being back where I started, with writing that is risky, daring, subversive, the writing "that most engages my heart and soul, the writing that is about families, parents, and children," in biography, oral history, autobiography, poetry.

My father is dead now, and whether he ever loved me or my writing enough is beyond change.... In writing about families, in cre-

ating and re-creating them, I rejoin the family of my own choosing.
I am part of them. They cannot throw me out; I take them in. I
write to remain a member of the human race, the family that en-
compasses us all.

The morning after I finished "Why I Write" my husband and
I saw films of the CT scan. We could not talk about the clenched-
fist white spot under his right eye, bigger than a golf ball, press-
ing against his brain. Indeed, we said very little on that very long
drive to school that morning, for the diagnosis was a malignant
brain tumor. "I'm prepared to die," he told me matter-of-factly.
"I want you to know I have no regrets about our marriage, all
29 years. None." Just as matter-of-factly I replied, gripping the
wheel so I wouldn't crack us up, "Well, I'm not prepared for
you to die, and I want you to fight this." And so I went to class,
with "zero at the bone" burning in my brain, to read the essay
that I decided to give my husband for his impending birthday.
We make our own presents, future or no.

My voice began trembling and my hands started shaking long
before we got to "Why I Write," which I saved for the very end.
The good reason for this was, of course, the pedagogical decision
not to take up too much class time with my own work. I cannot
remember what we said that day about Corbett and Aristotle on
invention. I think we talked that day about Eudora Welty's concept of *confluence* in *One Writer's Beginnings,* and Tess Gallagher's
"My Father's Love Letters" and the *Paris Review* interview with
Thurber: "I'm always writing. I write even at parties. Sometimes
my wife looks over at me and says, 'Dammit Thurber, stop writing' " (96).

Finally I took a deep breath and told the class about how I
wrote the essay, that it had taken all my life and one week and
would take more. I know I did not tell them about the CT scan.
I know also that although I am usually careful to make eye
contact with my students and to vary the pace of my presentation
and allow for interruptions and relevant digressions and questions, I clung to the paper and without looking at anyone read
the essay straight through in one gulp. There were tears in my
eyes as I finished, as indeed there are as I write again about this
day of days, and there was silence in that room.

No one said anything, but the time was up anyway. On their
way out, however, several of the students said it was a good class,

some shook my hand, and one gave me a hug. That had never before happened so early in the semester. It was like leaving church.

For the rest of the term I heard about that class, from the students in person and in their notebooks. In risk taking, risk teaching, showing them how much I cared about writing, I had complicated their lives. They had to care too. A writing center tutor wrote, "All over Richmond I run into lynn bloom [sic] students moaning about their papers—they all want to put a lot into it; they feel the paper is demanding a lot of them." A former bass player corroborated: "Damn you, Lynn Bloom. Have you let me in for a life of writing, for a life of struggle to create, to express, to move from a state of knowing less to a state of knowing more or less what I want to say?"

Nevertheless, the class was, as one student said, "charged up and full of energy." The novelist observed: "Here I am on a dismal rainy day, with my family life falling apart (and yes that makes me cranky, yes that makes it harder to get something done) *and this class cheers me up* and helps me believe I am a writer." Another analyzed her experience as a graduate student in this way:

> Although I went through four years of college and possess a bachelor's degree [in business administration], I am attending college for the very first time. . . . I am now in school for the sole purpose of learning and I can't seem to get enough. . . . For the first time ever I have understood the idea of getting satisfaction from the project itself rather than concentrating on the grade.

A first-time composition teacher, whose term project was research on "ways to make students care about their writing," said:

> There is an atmosphere where everyone cares about their writing. . . . I have tried to think back over what may have prompted this atmosphere in our class. . . . It was Lynn Bloom's reading her paper on why she writes. She took so many chances in that paper—invested so much confidence in our class—went out on a limb to make us feel like we were a gathering of writers with whom she wanted to share her work. [Before that] the risk had gone out of my writing . . . but when I heard her read, and when I heard some of the other students' papers, I realized that this class was going to take a differ-

ent turn from my other graduate classes, and that maybe it was going to give me the ability to earn the distinction of calling myself a writer.

There's not much more to say. Through taking risks, through letting my students see me as a writer-always-in-process who cares deeply about what I write, and can admit vulnerability and change, I effected a paradigm shift. Within two months' time, my class had changed from students in the process of learning about teaching in order to teach writing to students in the process of becoming writers in order to teach writing. They learned about teaching writing as they wrote, and as they read—research essays, finally Lindemann, and each others' writings—while they wrote. As a student writer-in-process said, "I am grateful that the class was structured (de-structured?) to allow us to answer our own questions." Another exulted, "[This] has turned out to be a writing boot camp for me." Even the single holdout, the elementary teacher who never wanted to write, succumbed to the new paradigm within a month:

I surrender! I'm just going to let myself be surprised with the directions this class takes. Risky voyages can take you where you never thought of going. Safe voyages are limited. Dr. Bloom has decided on the risky voyage and I admire her courage for picking it. I can be game enough to cast off my mooring ropes ("But I thought this class was supposed to . . . ") and sail on down the river with her.

In becoming writers, the class was becoming a community of writers as well. The depth of their investment in their own writing mirrored a receptivity to the work of their peers: "When [someone] reads a paper aloud, intelligent and instructive discussion follows. When a teaching problem is presented . . . we solve it as a class and we learn." Thus the students' engagement with "Why I Write" and their own emerging commitment to writing (two-thirds of them enrolled, the next semester, in my graduate workshop in Writing Nonfiction, including the formerly resistant teacher), to each other, and to teaching writing enabled me, two weeks later, to tell them that if I had to miss class because of my husband's impending surgery and its potentially terrifying aftermath, they could teach themselves until I returned. Just as they were already doing.

The operation was swift, the outcome sweet. The surgeon's

grin stretched above his mask when he came to give me the news. He repeated, over and over, what a lucky man my husband was. My own good luck was obvious. The biopsy revealed that the cyst the doctor had just removed was the most benign of possibilities, composed of the same cells that form teeth, and the most rare—so rare that he might encounter only one such case in his career. But although the surgeon has since become a kind friend, he could not know then, or even now, how doubly lucky I have been in finding a new voice as a writer and a new paradigm of teaching writing teachers, themselves a new family, as I have weathered this watershed experience.

CODA

After my husband's good health had remained stable for a year, I finally had enough perspective on the class and on my own still-emerging commitment to the risky realm of belletristic writing to attempt this essay. I had put it off as long as I could, but I had agreed to read it at a professional meeting—my first public appearance in my private voice in fifty years—and the deadline was fast approaching. From the safe distance of time and a move to Connecticut, I began to wonder whether I was romanticizing the experience, investing it with as much of an impact on the students as it had on me. There was only one way to find out.

I sent the sixth draft to the students, and on a rainy March afternoon went to Virginia to find out. "Did I get it right?" They knew I was as vulnerable to them then as I had been the year before, and as we huddled together in a small room in the writing center it was clear that they had remained a community of writers and teachers and that they regarded me as part of that community. "Yes," they said, it reflected both the letter and the spirit of our class—which they demonstrated over and over again as they told me about their teaching and their own writing.

My students were teaching their students to write the way their experience told them that real writers learn to write. "Writers read a lot," they said, "and pick up vocabulary and sentence patterns, a sense of style, as they read." "Writers learn from reading aloud, paying attention to the sound." "Writers learn from copying texts by hand as Corbett recommends, from getting the feel of their sentences, from imitating texts." "They learn from writing and revising work that really means something to them, and from submitting multiple drafts for portfolio grading." "Writers learn from reading their works to each other." "Writers learn from teachers who write, who are part of a group of writers."

Indeed, my students were real writers, in process and in product. Two students had switched from the M.A. to the M.F.A. program in creative writing. One student was trying, with some frustration, to control his sprawling style and vary his repetitive vocabulary. Another was in the process of transforming a collection of personal essays into a bildungsroman. A poet was experimenting with prose to see what he'd learn. The prize-winning novelist had completed another novel and won honorable mention in the AWP contest. And the most resistant student, the elementary school teacher, had edited a book of the uncollected writings of her favorite author, E. B. White, and submitted it to Harper & Row.

Another student, a high school teacher who took "Son of Paradigm Shift" last summer, told me simply, in a letter last fall, "you made me a writer. I'm getting up at 5 every morning to write for an hour before school." A letter in February said that on the strength of an essay he'd written about fatherhood, he had been invited to become a magazine home repair columnist. In May, his short story won first prize in the Writer's Federation of Nova Scotia contest.

I have begun the most difficult writing of my life, about my life and the lives of others close, distant, compelling. It's risky, but exhilarating, to invest so much and care so much, but there is no other choice. I have been invited to share drafts not only with my students—one kind of community—but with an informal network of essayists—another community, whose work is so good that the prospect of their criticism terrifies me. There is no other choice here, either. For this is the way to find our voices, find our families, find ourselves.

WORKS CITED

Berg, Stephen, ed. *In Praise of What Persists.* New York: Harper, 1983.

Bloom, Lynn Z. "Why I Write." *Maryland English Journal* (Spring 1989).

Didion, Joan. "Why I Write." *The Writer on Her Work.* Ed. Janet

Sternburg. New York: Norton, 1980. 17–25.

Gallagher, Tess. "My Father's Love Letters." *In Praise of What Persists.* Ed. Stephen Berg. New York: Harper, 1983. 109–24.

Kuhn, Thomas. *The Structure of Scientific Revolutions.* 2nd ed. Chicago: U of Chicago P, 1970.

Lindemann, Erika. *A Rhetoric for Writing Teachers.* 2nd ed. New York: Oxford, 1987.

Orwell, George. "Why I Write." *The Orwell Reader.* New York: Harcourt, 1956. 390–96.

Plimpton, George, and Max Steele. "James Thurber." *Writers at Work: The Paris Review Interviews.* Ed. Malcolm Cowley. New York: Viking, 1959. 83–98.

Welty, Eudora. *One Writer's Beginnings.* Cambridge, MA: Harvard UP, 1984.

Wiesel, Elie. "Why I Write: Making No Become Yes." *New York Times Book Review* 14 April 1985. Rpt. *The Essay Connection.* Ed. Lynn Z. Bloom. 2nd ed. Lexington, MA: Heath, 1988. 22–27.

Dedicated, with love and respect, to my English 636 ("Teaching Composition") class at Virginia Commonwealth University, Fall 1987: Sara Brown, Linda Burmeister, Linda Christian, Becky Dale, Christian Gehman, Warren Hayman, Karen Johnston, Joan Lanzillotti, Jay Looney, Mark Morrison, Kathleen Reilly, Dana Smith, Judy Taylor, Karen Weatherspoon; and to my husband, Martin Bloom.

6

Dialogue Across
the Two Cultures

CHARLES MORAN AND WILLIAM J. MULLIN

*Charles Moran and William J. Mullin both teach at the University
of Massachusetts at Amherst. Moran, a professor of English, is
Director of the University Writing Program, and Mullin, a professor of Physics, directs the university's Junior Year Writing Program. Moran recently co-edited, with Elizabeth Penfield, a book
titled* **Contemporary Critical Theory and the Teaching of Literature** *and is currently investigating the effects of computer technology on the writing classroom. Mullin, a condensed matter
theorist, is interested in the quantum mechanics of liquid and solid
helium. He is co-author, with J. J. Brehm, of* **Introduction to the
Structure of Matter.**

When asked to write a collaborative chapter for this book, we
decided to write in dialogue, using Bitnet communication (a kind
of electronic mail) to exchange views about our own practice and
experience, both as writers and teachers of writing, in two different disciplines. We focused on two related questions: How
did our early writing experiences inform our teaching of writing?
And, How did our two disciplines—Physics and English—shape
our experiences as writers and as teachers of writing?

We find, not surprisingly, that we are different: partly, a result
of individual styles; partly, discipline related. Yet there is cer-

tainly common ground, both in the ways we go about our own writing and the ways we present writing to our students.

Charlie:

As a writing teacher, I have always felt that the student writer must somehow be connected to the writing. Without this connection, all is sound and fury. Therefore, when I find a student connected to a subject, I break all the rules: permit student writers to miss deadlines, conflate assignments. As long as the writer is engaged, connected to the writing, I feel happy. My best imaginable class is one in which I sit silently while student writers write.

The roots of this pedagogy are to be found, I believe, in my early writing experiences—chiefly academic or "school" writing, unpleasant and unproductive, when I wrote papers because I had to. One of these disasters I remember with an awful clarity. At St. George's School, in the twelfth grade, we were assigned a senior English term paper. We had to present a topic on week one, an outline on week two, a rough draft on week four, and a final draft on week six. I wrote the rough draft on the night before it was due, on a topic that is still burned into my memory: "Hemingway's Use of Nada in his Fiction." I can't remember where I found the topic, but I do remember writing all night, alone, in an empty classroom, in Diman Hall. By morning I had enough writing to satisfy the teacher. I've not liked Hemingway since.

From the same course I remember also a good writing experience. I was given an open-ended topic and wrote a piece describing night fishing with my father on Lake Champlain. The writing wasn't easy, but I kept at it and felt at the end that it was pretty close to what I wanted. I liked what I had written. The piece was published in *The Dragon,* the school literary magazine, in the Prize Day 1954 issue. It is worth noting that *The Dragon* travels with me, secure in my publications file. I've not read "A Night on the Lake" for thirty years, but I keep it. I left the Hemingway essay in my wastebasket when I left the school.

I find in these writing experiences the ground for my belief that writers need to feel connected to their subject. To encourage this "connection" in my classes, I stay away from assigned topics and prescriptive formats like those of my Hemingway paper. I don't teach the term paper, because this ersatz genre carries with it so much that can inhibit real writing. Instead, I encourage open-ended topics like the one that led me to "A Night on the Lake," which made writing of value to me.

Assigned topics that I do give are meant as prompts, a means of starting the writer in some direction, not a means of limiting or restricting fields. Because I turn the choice of subject, and implicitly the problem of connection, over to my students, I try to teach them how to connect to a given subject or discover a subject to which they already have a connection. "Imagine that you face this particular issue (e.g., whether or not to approve of an abortion) in your own family" may lead the writer toward personal, rather than abstract, implication in the issue—one kind of connection. Or, "Imagine that you are explaining X about this subject to person Y" may lead the writer toward an imagined rhetorical context, and therefore to another kind of connection.

Bill:

I agree that the presence of an emotional connection is absolutely necessary for a successful writing experience, but for me something more is also needed: an intellectual connection that comes from knowing my subject matter well.

I began to find this out in high school—from a bad experience. I was asked to produce the senior class history (1952) for inclusion in the yearbook. I had no idea how to construct interesting descriptions of the Fathers and Sons Banquet (which, I recall, I hadn't actually attended), or the football team's losing season. I remember the result as fairly humiliating to my writing reputation. (I have just reread this masterpiece and am not mistaken in my assessment.) How should I have attacked this task? Perhaps with humor; but that would have been undignified. Better, I should have interviewed my classmates and found out what the class history really was. No wonder I could not write it; I didn't know it.

Perhaps I began to make some progress in this regard as a graduate student at Washington University. There I took an atomic physics course with Edward Condon, a well-known author and editor, who assigned a term paper that had only one real requirement besides a word count: to include at least three references that were not in English. Despite this vague assignment, I made a connection to the topic. I read all the relevant background material—in German—and reported on an interesting experiment that tested the hypothesis that energy might be conserved only on average and not in detail. My essay was solid because it was based on material I knew, understood. I had overcome my usual problem of not digging for or creating enough information. Physics is probably the ultimate limit of this need for background work, since it is almost always 95 percent "research"—doing mathematical calculations or experiments—and only 5 percent writing in the traditional sense. Maybe that is why there is so much bad scientific writing; it is often such a small part of the process that it is often viewed as unimportant.

Now, years later, I have published a number of theoretical physics papers and have co-authored a large text on modern physics. Those experiences lead me to agree, Charlie, that connectivity is vital—intellectual as well as emotional. Unless I have done the research that goes along with the writing, I'm writing nonsense off the top of my head. Notice I didn't say "that goes BEFORE the writing." Some of my bad pieces might have been useful if I had used them to tell me what I needed to learn and understand before I went on to a final draft.

The students in our Writing in Physics course[1] (part of the University's Junior Year Writing Program) often find themselves writing on topics with which they are unfamiliar. That is part of the point of the course—to introduce them to material at the frontiers of physics. Even though they are physics majors, many are still not involved with the subjects they are writing about. My own bad writing experiences, in which I tried to handle topics I was not involved with, convince me of the need to include some assignments that gear themselves to student interest. To facilitate this, I often break my habit of specifying subject, audience, and style for assignments and let the students choose. Despite a substantial knowledge hurdle, most students usually find some topics or styles with which they resonate, occasionally with remarkable results.

Charlie:
Bill, we do overlap on the need for connection, even if you emphasize knowing your subject and I emphasize caring about

[1] A description of this course appears in my article "Writing in Physics," *The Physics Teacher* 27 (1989): 342–348.

it. I do agree that knowing is important: the material for my essay "A Night on the Lake" was autobiographical, so I did know that subject; and the Hemingway paper was, perhaps you'd say, meaningless to me because I didn't know enough about Hemingway? Or literary criticism? Clearly, there's a relationship here between caring and knowing about a subject. It would be hard to know which comes first. I have a feeling that in English we tend to highlight the caring, and in physics you tend to highlight the knowing. Or perhaps we're both talking about the same thing but using different language to express it. Clearly, as writing teachers we do agree: students need to be permitted, and encouraged, to write about subjects they know and care about.

However, I remember a time when knowing, or at least the activity I called "research," became a kind of avoidance behavior for me. I should have started writing sooner than I did—*before* I knew what I was writing about. In a graduate course at Brown University I wrote a paper on "Milton's Chaos in *Paradise Lost*," which the professor thought I could expand into a Master's thesis. I agreed. So off I went to the library and collected more and more information on possible sources for Milton's particular treatment of Chaos. I kept the results in file boxes of six-inch by four-inch note cards, which piled up in a gratifying way. When I sat down to write the thesis, however, I found that I really didn't have anything to say. The note taking and research had assumed a momentum of their own; the research had *not* served a clear purpose. I did finish the thesis, but it wasn't something I was proud of. I have kept other work that I did then, but not this. The thesis, and the note cards, are somewhere in a Providence landfill.

Contrast this, Bill, with your class history. You were writing without sufficient information; I was buried by mine. This experience, and others like it, lead me to teach prewriting strategies in my writing classes. I encourage students to try out the "write-first-then-think" model, not the "think-first-then-write" model that is still presented by most handbooks and, come to think of it, was probably what doomed my Hemingway paper. In my classes, the "research paper" becomes the "documented essay"— one where you write until you need more knowledge—and then, after writing, you go looking for the information you need, perhaps in the library. And, as you know, we've proceeded in this way, you and I, as we've written this article. The happy result: we generated a tremendous amount of material and then did the chainsaw-pruning needed to bring it all under some measure of control.

Bill:

Earlier, I said that physics is only about 5 percent writing: the creation of the research article. But that estimate neglects a great deal of writing of a nontraditional kind—what you in composition call *prewriting* and *writing-to-learn*—that we usually lump into the term *research.* I think that the nature of the research process, at least in theoretical physics, may have implications concerning the teaching of physics and, in particular, in the use of writing to teach physics.

Let me illustrate by examining how a typical theoretical physicist—that's me—proceeds on a research project. Suppose I am interested in calculating T_1, the spin-lattice relaxation time for polarized ^{3}He (pronounced *helium-three*) gas. First—after doing sufficient background reading, of course—I might do some back-of-the-envelope calculation, which in this case was given to me by Mike Richards, an English collaborator on this project. This is a simple mathematical and verbal argumentation that gives me an idea of what I might expect as an answer. This step is perhaps a form of prewriting.

My next step is to find some rigorous formalism, in this case the Boltzmann equation, that allows me to derive, by a long-winded mathematical argument, an expression for T_1. To gain even more insight, I need to carry out numerical computations based on the formula and express those numbers graphically. From these various forms I can see that T_1 has an interesting behavior in large magnetic fields. This is a new prediction some experimentalist could test one day. From the literature, I know there is another known property that my result confirms. It was first shown back in 1975 by a Canadian chemist, but my method of derivation shows that his interpretation of *why* it occurs is incorrect. I now see the real reason—and the reason has some nice "physics" (intuitive understanding) in it—in simple enough form to express it verbally. Now I'm ready to do "the 5 percent activity," that is, writing the article that tells the world of physics what I have uncovered concerning T_1. Of course, it does more than just this; it presses me to think through the entire project once more and refine the calculations and interpretation of results.

Note that the physics understanding exists on at least four distinct levels. There is my rigorous formula, which is accurate but arcane. The formula's meaning must be interpreted, first, in simpler mathematics via the quick back-of-the-envelope calculation. I extract further information by numerical and graphical analysis. Finally, and no less importantly, I need to express the ideas in words. I see the creation of all these forms as involving *writing*—expressive activities that generate ideas and convey information.

The nature of the research process as recounted above does connect to the way I teach physics. In most courses we give problem assignments to induce active learning behavior on the part of students. In elementary courses students find the right formulae and work out numerical solutions; the activity is a (weak) analog of my research's numerical analysis. In advanced courses we often assign simple versions of the rigorous mathematical derivation. However, students rarely do activities that parallel the back-of-the-envelope calculation or the verbal interpretation. These constitute the intuitive inner life of physics— but we don't require them of students!

Physics skills necessarily span both math and language skills. If you discuss a subject but can't put it into a mathematical formulation, you're not doing physics. On the other hand, if you can't put your mathematical derivation into some form of plain English, you haven't really understood it. Richard Feynman used to test how deeply he had understood an idea in physics by whether he could explain it to the general public. Once he was asked to give an explanation of the connection between spin and statistics (never mind what that means). He agreed, but came back later saying he couldn't—not because it was too complicated for the nonspecialist, but rather because he realized that physicists did not yet understand the concept well enough. His book *QED* is a perfect example of his conviction that extraordinarily complicated physical concepts can often be made beautifully clear with just words and pictures.

When I teach physics majors, I often ask students to write essays (usually short ones) using mainly words instead of equations on a variety of basic concepts in the course. In my senior quantum mechanics course, a several-page essay written on Bell's theorem, directed to other seniors and containing little math, plunges students into the depths of the differences between quantum logic and common sense. Writing is almost imperative to develop an understanding of this profound and weird subject. When I teach our department's Writing in Physics course, I assign three- to four-page essays that require nonmathematical explanations of topics like Heisenberg's uncertainty relation or how an airplane flies.

I would also like students to learn to write material that integrates both the mathematical and the verbal argumentation. Since student problem solvers almost always leave out the words, perhaps I should demand in my nonwriting physics courses that some of the problem homeworks be written carefully in an integrated fashion that includes verbal interpretation. That is something I have yet to try. I bet the students won't like it.

Charlie:

Bill, your description of your research in physics makes me realize how important collaboration is in your field. In a sense, you are writing to your team, composed of fellow physicists, and it's in their interest to help the team produce the best possible result. Certainly I find writing collaboratively—as we are now doing—a new and pleasant experience. Generally we humanists write, like monks in their cells, or in library carrels, alone. In the last two years, we in the Writing Program have developed a reading group, where we share works-in-progress, both for criticism and support. It looks to me as if you-all in physics have been working and, to an extent, writing like this for years.

Bill:

Collaborative writing does seem to be a hot topic in composition theory circles, but as you correctly point out we physicists have been doing this kind of thing all along; we just didn't give it a name. A recent important paper in the most prestigious physics journal has 225 authors, but that is the product of an accelerator "factory" and is not a typical physics collaboration.

Last year I took part in a more typical case. I had published a short paper proposing an experiment. A close friend and colleague, Brian Cowan at the University of London, read my paper and suggested a way to measure the same thing by a different technique. However, we needed to do some more theoretical work to predict what might be observed in an experiment. Brian worked out the first rough cut of the theory and sent me his notes. I continued where they left off, reduced the calculation to the point of necessary numerical work, and did the computations.

Time to write the paper: Brian wrote the introduction and the background theory and faxed me the results. I felt that his writing was a little too concise. I rewrote his part, expanding it and—to my mind at least—improving it. I then added the rest of the methodology and a summary of the numerical results, including some graphs. I faxed that to him. He liked what I had done with his part but felt that some of my writing could be made clearer. He rewrote my sections and faxed that back to me. I retyped it all and sent the completed article to a journal. During all this we had kept in close contact by Bitnet. At every level the resulting work was much better than either of us could have done individually.

It would be interesting to include more group activity and group writing in my classes. It would be unusual. While students are usually paired off in lab experiments, even then they write separate lab reports. I do encourage students to work on homework problem assignments together. If we consider solving physics problems as a kind of writing, as I have argued, then my students are writing collaboratively—even though they end up handing in separate and not joint homework.

So far, I have not incorporated other collaborative assignments into my Writing in Physics course. While students use peer review extensively, it has not gone much beyond that. But why not have, say, one pair- or group-assignment out of the six or so in a semester? The problem is to insure the teaming of individuals who can really benefit from the joint effort. I know that I cannot collaborate with everyone; the chemistry—I mean the physics—has to be just right.

Both:

So at the end of a dialogue: a brief chorus, or duet. Both of us write, and write a great deal. Both of us use writing in the early stages of our work as we define and work through a problem. Both of us write well when we feel a personal connection to our subject. Both of us work collaboratively—in the writing of this essay and, generally, in our other professional work.

We find that our experience and practice as writers form the basis for what we say and do as writing teachers. We would hope that such a connection between personal experience and pedagogical practice would be not the exception but the rule.

II

INSIGHTS

*. . . teaching what we've
learned on the job: as
editors, from editors, in
writing groups, from critics
and mentors*

7

Writing and Teaching Writing

RICHARD MARIUS

Richard Marius has been Director of the Expository Writing Program at Harvard University since 1978. He is the author of three novels, biographies of Martin Luther and Thomas More, and several textbooks about writing, including the widely acclaimed A Writer's Companion, *now in its second edition. He writes the book column for* Harvard Magazine *and contributes regularly to professional journals.* Once in Arcadia, *his latest novel, is scheduled for publication in early 1991.*

In a crowded taxi bouncing toward the Seattle airport under darkly overcast skies after the CCCC meeting in 1989, Mimi Schwartz came up with the topic for this essay: What have I learned from being a writer about teaching students how to write?

I was reluctant because I am too obscure a writer to set myself up as an example to anybody. But maybe that is not the point. Most of us are obscure. Obscure or not, we live in a world where writing is not only indispensable but idealized. Once on a lark after a somewhat drunken meal at an MLA meeting in Washington, a raucous group of us lined up to have our palms read by a fortune teller we spied near the restaurant in Georgetown. She told me that I was a writer. I was impressed. Later an old friend on hearing this marvelous tale said, "Marius, she was completely safe; anybody in our society who writes a letter to his Aunt Minnie thinks he's a writer and that with enough time he could produce a book that would sell more copies than *Gone with the Wind*." Somehow his cynical words encouraged me; if writing is a universal fantasy, maybe our students share it, and maybe we can teach them something.

One thing is certain: most of our students will have to write sustained, thoughtful prose to advance in their jobs. The committee meetings, the conference calls, the business lunches, the quiet conversations in offices, the shouted exchanges on construction sites all must be turned into writing if they are to have lasting effect. In many professions, the future may lie in the hands of those able to write the best reports.

But beyond professional demands, a prodigious longing to put words on paper rolls through our society. Uncountable numbers of people keep journals. Manuscripts pour into magazines and publishing houses. When I am asked the supremely Northeastern question, "What do you *do?*" (distinct from the standard Southern question of my youth, "Where are you *from?*") and I answer that I write, I almost invariably get the response, "I have a book I've been wanting to write," or, "I have always wanted to write." That is what the fortune teller in Georgetown knew. Occasionally people tell me how much they still hate a writing teacher they had years—even decades—ago. I suspect that part of their enduring anger may be born of frustration: "I wanted to learn something important, and my teacher didn't teach me."

I have been writing for the public since I was fifteen years old, when I went to work for a little semiweekly newspaper in a small Tennessee town six miles from the farm where I grew up. I have been teaching writing since I decided in 1970 that my history students at the University of Tennessee could not learn anything about history unless they knew how to write about it. The traditional mode of the teaching historian was to cover as many facts as possible and make students repeat them on exams. I found that they forgot the facts as soon as the exams were over, but they remembered papers they wrote. More important, writing taught them the fundamental meaning of the Greek word *historeo,* to inquire, to question, from which we derive our word *history*. I dropped mid-terms and finals and turned my course into a workshop for writing about history. Writing was important to me; I wanted to make it important for my students.

I tried to teach them what I learned from thinking about my own writing. Since 1978 I have been doing much the same thing as Director of the Expository Writing Program at Harvard, charged with giving the only course required of all Harvard students.

Some insights are personal. Writing is an intimate act done for public consumption. I never knew a writer who did not yearn for approval. Yet I have to guard myself and my teachers from the propensity to get angry with students because they write badly or because they can't spell or because their papers look sloppy or because they don't number their pages or because they can't put four sentences together. Why the anger?

Many teachers of composition respond to student writing— especially poor student writing—as some sort of aggression. "This vile little twit thinks he can put this piece of *garbage* over on *me*!" Such teachers respond as if the student has walked across a deadline, ignoring the "danger of death" signs. The teacher draws a red pen and shoots to kill.

Unless we treat students as colleagues to be helped rather than as Philistines to be slain, we can never teach them anything. Yes, a student may have written a thoughtless, stupid paper that any half-literate imbecile can recognize for what it is—not worth a teacher's time. Yet there it is—the student's mind, spread out for everyone to see as in that scene in the movie M*A*S*H where the shower tent collapses around poor Hot Lips Hoolihan, leaving her naked to the world. Writers are naked once they have written, and even if they have been lazy or slovenly, they are helpless before the eye of the audience and deserve compassion.

Every writer calculates—and partly miscalculates—the audience. Student writers may go to extremes. They think of the audience as the teacher—a stuffy automaton demanding sincere verbiage, complicated sentences, no contractions, no first or second person pronouns. Or else they suppose the audience to be their friends in the bar, ready to laugh at cute remarks or vulgar jokes and react feelingly to sentiment. To the teacher, either attitude may seem like a challenge requiring a counterattack. "Do you think I'm so dull that I like pedantry like this?" Or, "Do you think I'm some slang-ridden teenager?"

The experienced writer may miscalculate as badly. He or she supposes an audience that is a secret inner self, an imagined doppelgänger, an intellectual twin—patient, eager, and loving. I crouch over my keyboard here, staring into my screen most often very late at night, the street outside silent and the house asleep, and I write as though the computer screen were a sort of mirror. By looking into it, I seek the self that both creates my work and appreciates it. I work hard to please that second self—revising, straining for the right word, shortening or lengthening sentences, changing, changing, changing. Somewhere in my mind is a Platonic ideal of what is *right* for my prose; here in the screen my reality stretches towards my ideal.

Finally I must put a manuscript into the mail. That is always a bad day. A fearsome awakening comes: This *thing* will be read by strangers. If the work is a book, reviews appear. Every writer gets some bad reviews. I know writers who say bad reviews don't bother them. They lie. Some claim never to read reviews good or bad; I suspect they lie, too; if not, I regret their cowardice.

The unfair reviews sting. When my biography of Thomas More came out in 1984, it went through five printings. Most reviewers liked it. But some slammed my work, furious because I did not make More the character Paul Scofield played in "A Man for All Seasons." The More of stage and screen was calmly heroic and wished no ill to any man; the More I found in the records roared against Protestants, and in thousands of blistering pages urged that the government burn them at the stake.

Some Catholic reviewers attacked the book as though it were the Antichrist, and many of their assaults were personal. Behind most of these criticisms was the supposition that I had an ulterior purpose in writing the biography, a malicious desire to damn what multitudes of right-thinking people have praised. During the years I was working on the book I felt no such motives; like my students, I was trying my best to get it right.

When I am teaching—especially when I am bending with my pencil over a student paper like a surgeon holding a scalpel over a living body—I try to remember my bad reviews. I try to read the paper for what is there and to seek whatever it is the student is trying to say and to assume the best of all possible motives. I try never to be the old-fashioned schoolmaster who sees every error as a disciplinary problem for which the best solution is a good caning. If a writing teacher remembers anything, it should be the first injunction of the Hippocratic oath: Do no harm.

And yet to teach is to judge. I have never had any patience with teachers who see writing as a therapy session where the object is to make students feel good. I want my students to feel good because they do well, not because I pretend that their work is better than it is. Students see through our little hypocrisies. For a long time we tried to run our writing center at Harvard on the counseling model cherished by two directors. Conferences had to be an hour long. The tutors were not to be authorities; they were to coax students into being their own critics and to send them on their way with the sense of having been loved.

Our statistics were dismal. A few students loved the steady praise of their work. Most did not. In a good year about 200 students came to the center; few returned after one visit. In my informal talks around the university, I found that the general sentiment of our students was that the writing center was a good place to go if you needed another mother. Most students did not.

In selecting my third writing center director, I took as a model my own editor of twenty years. She has never tried to rewrite my work; but she has always given me an honest reaction as a friend trying to help me do better. She assumes that I have something worth saying, but she never pretends that everything I write is almost perfect. She tells me when she likes something and when she does not. She tells me when she thinks my tone is wrong or when I repeat myself or when I don't give enough evidence or when I go on pouring evidence over a point that does not need any more. She sometimes suggests a new approach. When she dislikes something, she says so cautiously and in detail—never with an ugly word scrawled in the margins. She asks relentless questions, "What do you mean? Why are you doing this?" She reacts as a good reader and a friend who has read my work closely, knows it well enough to talk about it fluently, and cares enough for me to treat it professionally. We both want it to come out right.

I want to be that kind of editor to my students—a careful and honest reader, letting them know that I *want* them to succeed but that I have problems with how they have gone about their work, sometimes suggesting a new approach. I assume that they have something to say—even if I think they have written the paper a couple of hours before turning it in. We try to find it together.

In choosing a new director for our writing center, I chose another writer, Dr. Linda Simon, author of five books and several hundred book reviews. The tutors under her supervision never put a mark on the papers they read, but they read them critically and speak frankly but not harshly about them. To a student with a problem paper their attitude is something like this: "You have something to say; you have not said it well yet; why don't you try it again? Maybe you should try this." In consequence, we now have nearly 500 students a year using the writing center, and students come back for session after session with the tutors.

A strange kind of mystique seems to be building up in the CCCC and in composition circles in general. It is that the teacher should not be an authority figure. Authority figures are supposed to be bad for student health. This notion is nonsense; an authority is not necessarily a tyrant. If our experience does not give us some authority, what good has it been? Every writer encounters authority in bosses, editors, and other readers. Write a disorganized, dull, opinionated report vital to your job and the work of your business or profession, and you will get a dose of authority fast in the annoyance and even contempt of your peers and superiors. We owe it to our students to give them the benefit of our experience. That means sometimes saying, "Well, I'm sorry, but if you say all abortionists are murderers without even trying to understand their view, you will insult many of your readers and they will think you are a fanatic, and normal people do not pay any attention to fanatics."

It is a commonplace of modern critical theories that no one can write without assuming a tradition and that no one can read without bringing to any text everything that she has read before. Writing and reading take place within customs long established and slow to change. Obviously there are variations within the tradition. An essay by Joan Didion can scarcely be taken for one by Henry James. But the similarities of good essays are far greater than the differences whether the essayist is Cicero on old age or Annie Dillard on the death of a frog. When instead of participating in this tradition, the student flies off into tedious clichés or fallacious logic or opinionated generalizations, we must say so—gently but firmly and without ambiguity, for readers will not accept such stuff.

Once we comment on papers, we must let students revise them. Someone at a recent CCCC said that a teacher's comments on a paper that can't be revised are nothing but an autopsy report.

Every writer knows that writing is drafting. At an early time in my life I discovered the pleasure of typing the same page over and over again until it came out "right." I learned to type when I was a young adolescent. I found a sensual pleasure in pecking away at the keyboard of an old, heavy-bodied Royal

Standard typewriter, bought for fifty dollars from my high school typing teacher after it had already served two years as the anvil for the hammering fingers of students. It rests on the floor, not five feet away as I write. I fondly call it the "black beast," and when I am stuck, I sometimes go back to it. My fingers may outrun my mind on the computer. The resisting springs of the black beast slow me down.

Typing pages over and over created several good habits. It made me weigh—if only for a split second—every word I used. It made me see more clearly the connections between one part of my piece and another. It made me see the piece again and again as a whole.

I do not believe that most of my students reread their first drafts. They will reread their own work and our comments if those comments aim at helping them do the next draft better. And we must give them time to revise. When I started teaching writing, I showered my students with writing assignments— sometimes eight papers a semester. But can a writer write that much? Any writer able to produce four finished essays in four months is a prodigy. How can we expect our students to do more? I recently spoke with a student who burst into tears because she said she had to write so many papers during a term that she didn't have a chance to do any of them well. She made an important point.

I require four essays a semester in my course. Each paper is from eight to ten pages long. I require two drafts of every paper. I mark them rigorously for evidence, content, form, and logic. I tell my students that I will read every draft they will write. I grade each draft anew. Real writers are judged by their last draft; why don't we allow the same privilege to our students? Why should we tell them that if they don't get it right the first time, we will average the grades on their various drafts? I never get it right the first time. The last ghosts of puritanism lurk in the gloomy shadows of composition courses. "By God," the ghosts cackle, "if the sinful little wretches don't get it right, make them suffer! Those who get a second chance should pay for it with tears of repentance, confessing that their punishment is just!" If we must be puritanical, why do we fixate on the puritan teaching of judgment day? Why not instead accept the puritan work ethic and give the greatest rewards to those who work longest and hardest?

Most of my students write with computers, and revision is

much easier for them than it was for previous writerly genera-
tions—as it is for all of us. They tell me that my comments are
helpful. They mean, I think, that my comments help them revise.
I think my comments are helpful because they create the sense
that the text is never finished, that it is always a fluid or semifluid
mass that the writer can change and reshape. Even more important is the reality of the kind of thinking that writing requires—detailed, orderly, and coherent thinking. Every writer
hits that place in a serious essay when she realizes that things
are not holding together well, that the evidence is not apt, or
that the conclusion is fuzzy. The solution is not to take a C and
go on to the next article; the writer knows that that article will
be in print somewhere until the earth falls into the sun. The
solution is to try again—and, if necessary, again and again and
again. My steady questioning of papers—combined with a grade
that indicates my judgment of the latest draft—motivates students to go back to their computers and revise again.

This business of thinking and writing has another side. Writing
should ripen. When I write a draft, put it up, think about it,
take it down a few days or a month or two months later, I can
add thoughts undreamed of during my first composition. We
need to space out our revisions in the classroom so that students
can get some distance from their work, incubate their ideas, and
come back for a fresh look at their own words.

As a writer, I am not much interested in teaching style. My
own style has taken years to develop. Style is like the arm of a
fastball pitcher; it keeps on developing long after the rest of the
person seems fully grown. Fool around with it too much when
the writer is too young and you may ruin it, making the writer
so self-conscious that he can't write easily, fluidly.

There are many acceptable styles in modern America. All too
often I find teachers belaboring their idiosyncratic preferences
in style to students who see those preferences violated in almost
everything they read. Yes, we can say, "Write this again; I don't
follow." Or, "Try to make this a little more direct." Students
usually improve when they try again. More than that is likely to
end in frustration for teacher and young writer alike. I am
amazed and appalled by writing teachers who nonchalantly tell
students, "Write this paper in a style appropriate for a popular
magazine and this one in a style appropriate for a scholarly
journal." The poor kids don't have the slightest idea what that
means; so they write for the popular magazine in a breezy, slangy

jargon that no editor would dream of printing, and they write for the scholarly journal with a pedantry that no one would dream of reading. A writing course based on style is doomed to failure. "My teacher gave me a C because she didn't like my style." The assumption here is that another teacher might have loved the style and that with the same work, the student might have received an A. The assumption is true.

I do wish my students wrote cleaner, leaner prose. One of my biggest frustrations as a teacher is to realize how they lack a sounding board in their heads that lets them hear their own sentences or see their own essays. Most writers I know have been avid readers since early childhood. I rarely have a student who reads for the pure joy of it.

Perhaps our students' unfamiliarity with reading is responsible for their wariness before anecdotes and facts they might weave into their own papers. Writers tell stories, and stories require details. My students shun both. Why?

I often give my students a collection of sources on the battles of Lexington and Concord. I say, "Tell me the story of what happened from the time the British troops left Boston on the evening of April 18 until they arrived back about twenty-four hours later." The sources swarm with detail. For example, a Minuteman at Lexington, one Sylvanus Wood, recalled years later that a British officer on horseback rode forward and shouted, "Lay down your arms, you damned rebels, or you are all dead men." According to British Lieutenant John Barker, the regulars had stood two hours knee-deep in a marsh at Cambridge, waiting for supplies they did not need, losing the vital element of surprise on which the operation depended, and then had marched about thirteen miles in their wet uniforms.

Here is a typical student version: "The British left Boston and marched to Lexington where they met a group of people. The British insulted them and shot at them and went on to Concord." Why do my students ignore the drama? Perhaps because they have so few times in their lives been stirred to dramatic excitement by what they have read. They have seen drama in video, but they have not had to use their imaginations to create drama from texts. They have not read enough themselves to see that we write to make readers relive our experience.

My students have taken enough exams to know that the chief requirement of the academic world is to avoid error. When we start to write specific facts, we can be wrong. Facts are slippery.

You have to check your sources to be sure you get the facts right. When you quote, you have to get the words straight and set them within your own writing in a way that does not jar. All that takes effort, and perhaps it requires an ideal created by a lifetime of reading stories, moved by them to feel the excitement and relive the drama of details. Most of my students prefer to make a summary statement that cannot be proved wrong. I want to teach them drama.

This writerly effort to share experience is not limited to the details of a story; it is also part of the thoughtful essay. The essayist wants to carry readers along with every turn of thought and across every logical bridge so that when we arrive together at a destination, we can say, "I know where we are and how we got there." Most of my students would rather tell me that they have indeed arrived at a destination, but they are unwilling to take the time to tell me how they got there. It is a commonplace of the writing trade nowadays to say that writing helps us think—but only if the writing describes step by step the progress of thought. Each of those steps is a story in itself that must be told with all the care the writer can summon. My students have seldom experienced the pleasures of following such thinking step by step through an essay; they have been taught to care only for what an essay concludes. We must teach them the steps.

The teacher's job will continue to be hard. Even so, in every semester that I teach, at least one student—and sometimes several—will come to the shining discovery that writing is possible. In every semester that I teach, I discover by reflecting on my own writing practice that I have something else to tell my students, some other help to offer them, perhaps a metaphor or some other words that help them see better what we are all trying to do.

In June 1988 I attended a baseball game at Fenway Park with some friends who brought their eight-year-old boy. The Red Sox won in a thrilling comeback, and the little boy began talking of the great baseball player he would be when he grew up. He looked at me and said, "Richard, if you could do anything in the world you wanted to do, what would it be?" I said, "Oh, I guess I'd write books and teach kids."

8

From Writer's Group to Class Workshop

KEN AUTREY

Ken Autrey pursues the writer's craft and the teacher's art at Francis Marion College in South Carolina, where he teaches advanced writing and a poetry writing workshop. He has published poetry and magazine features, as well as articles and reviews in professional journals. Having taught writing in various capacities for twenty years, Ken is now collaborating with Tom Waldrep on a composition textbook to be called **The Writer's Life.**

Henry Bowles stumbled into the Country Skillet, smiling vaguely at the brass bells which tinkled from the inside handle of the steel and glass door. He presented a single finger to the hostess who waddled toward him from the rear of the diner. She guided him to a greasy vinyl and formica booth, where Henry collapsed heavily, letting his head fall into weary hands.

This was the opening paragraph of "Kilgore Trout is Alive and Well," a story by Mike Taylor that inaugurated our writer's group in the spring of 1984. Mike's Kurt Vonnegut spinoff needed some work. But this moment marked a turning point in my writing and teaching, a revelation of sorts.

The seven or eight literati gathered in my den for that initial writer's group meeting were a mix of English Department grad students, faculty members, and other interested writers. Since Henry Bowles walked through that fictional door, most of the group's charter members have moved on—including Mike, whose freelance assignments have since taken him to Jamaica, the Baja Peninsula, and China and have led to several articles in *Sports Illustrated*.

Our group has ebbed, flowed, shrunk, grown, lain fallow, and flourished. Since it began, seventy or eighty writers—young and old, obsessed and flippant, published and unpublished, trembling and confident—have in their turn passed out drafts, sipped a cold beer, and sounded out to a rapt gathering of listeners. Twenty-three people appeared at one of our meetings—a runaway record in a packed living room. Occasionally we've had as few as two or three in attendance. And the constituents change from season to season. One spring produced a flowering of lyric poets. Last fall flushed out a flock of first novelists. Usually the meetings attract seven or eight and feature a nice mix of genres.

Back when several friends and fellow grad students proposed that we begin a writer's group, I consented immediately. But I felt uneasy and wasn't sure why. I knew nearly everyone invited to our first meeting, so I had no reason to hesitate. And as a teacher, I have for years insisted that students go public with their work in class. Why would I be reluctant to follow my own pedagogy?

In retrospect, I realize there were several reasons for my timidity. I had published articles in journals and newspapers and had presented conference papers, but I had doubts about my non-academic writing. And our group agreed from the outset that scholarly writing was out. The group would be open to stories, poems, essays, magazine articles, and segments of novels. But no critical analysis; no theory.

I was also spooked by the thought that these instant critics would be responding immediately to my work—without allowing the subtlety to sink in. I would be compelled to answer on the spot for what I had written. I could neither pack it off to an editor, like a message in a bottle, nor release it to the reading public to take flight or falter in obscurity. No, I would hear myself read it, and others would listen and comment. This was an experience my eighteen years of schooling had not prepared me for.

The truth is that I had usually worked alone, cloistered in my room, struggling to locate my own wavering frequency. I imagined myself, in Linda Brodkey's words, as "a solitary writer alone in a cold garret working into the small hours of the morning by the thin light of a candle" (396). I turned down the brightness of my computer screen when others approached. Over-the-shoulder readers seemed to me no better than back-seat drivers. The isolation chamber, the remote shack in the hills, the deepest recesses of the largest library: such work settings held great appeal for me. I was the one who slid my paper beneath the stack and hustled away from the teacher, fearful that she would read and grade it instantaneously.

But I dug out a poem, "October at the Beach," to read at our meeting. It was a brief, rather unambitious effort that had languished in my bottom drawer for a year or so. I guess I chose that one because I considered it finished—not very good, but finished. And it was safe: not too personal, not something I was struggling with currently. If my listeners didn't like it, I could toss it back in that bottom drawer and forget about it.

That night we first listened to and commented on Mike's story. Then Dot Thompson read one of her poems about Wheeler Hill, an old black neighborhood being whittled away by condominiums and tennis courts. Gordon Van Ness had brought a tale about a man named Farrington, an adventure with startling Beowulfian rhythms and overtones. Others also read from their work. I was both surprised by the quality of it all and impressed with the range of observations and suggestions that surfaced.

My turn came, and I read "October at the Beach," which begins,

The ocean's hunger
is what I notice, not
the old titanic cliches:
gulls and solitude
and floating bottles.

In the ensuing discussion, one or two participants noted cliches that, despite line three, had crept into the poem. There was an allusion to Icarus, for example, that in retrospect makes me cringe. As group reactions continued, I began to think the others took my work more seriously than I did. Then when someone asked where I planned to send the revised poem, I was sure of it. So I learned something at that first meeting: never solicit group comments on a piece that you believe is already finished or beyond redemption or shelved for good. Read something you feel strongly about, whatever its imperfections. I decided that if I trusted the others to be respondents as well as listeners, I should give them something I am actively working on.

There is a corollary to this principle—one that has some bearing on applying the writer's group approach to the classroom: if others take your work seriously, you're likely to invest more energy in it yourself. That is, it's possible for your respondents and critics to dramatize the importance of what you're doing, to make it come alive as real writing for a real audience. Our students particularly need this experience. This didn't happen with my poem because I had already relegated it to the past; I was too far away from it. For our next meeting—to be hosted by Mike—I resolved to bring something recent, something still taking shape.

What to write? My mind and desk were hopelessly cluttered with student papers and notes for several research projects. Driving home one day, in a sort of game with myself, I decided to grab the next unusual sight as the topic for an essay. I noticed a single shoe, a weathered brogan, on the side of the road. I had seen countless discarded shoes in my day but until then never gave them a thought. Suddenly, the possibilities hit me like a firehose, and I floored the accelerator, anxious to get home and isolate myself with our IBM Selectric. The resulting uncharacteristic spillage of ideas and ink became "Sole Searching," in which I speculate on how the shoes that litter our highways get there. I conclude that "if we could somehow delve into their histories, these subliminal blurs on our roads could prove to be windows to our national sole."

Group reactions to this essay were congenial if not enthusiastic. I raked in the suggestions like so many poker chips and a few days later tried my luck in placing the revised version with the local Sunday newsmagazine. The editor took it.

Without the Writer's Group, I would never have written "Sole

Searching." I realized that this band of committed writers and critics could motivate me. I had long since assumed that real writers write for real audiences, which I had repeated like a mantra for my students. But now this incantation took on new meaning.

I began to consider the implications of this revelation for the writing classes I was teaching. Our class workshop sessions had most often taken the form of peer group work, for which I would organize students in clusters of four or five, with instructions for reading and responding. Or, I would have individuals read portions of their completed or nearly completed papers to the class, asking then for reactions. I had kept this rather spontaneous and had made these activities tangential to other concerns of the class.

The Writing Group persuaded me that student work should be central to the course, and I began to designate students to bring in drafts each week, with enough copies for everyone. Each featured writer reads a draft aloud. We then take a couple minutes to review it silently, formulating questions and responses before launching into class discussion. I continue to use peer groups on occasion, but the total concentration of class energy on one piece at a time has heightened the value of workshop sessions, partly because when students know twenty other writers will read and carefully critique a draft, they are compelled to take their work seriously and hone it for an audience of peers.

In the several years since our group was organized, I have learned not only new procedures but lessons about writing that I have attempted to apply to my teaching. For example, I have found that when you read something of your own to others and ask for their comments, you relinquish some control over it. One evening I read the group a poem called "High Jumping," based on my memory of a high jumping bar some friends and I constructed when we were young. I imagined that years afterward my father had recycled the same materials as a trellis for his bean vines. I liked the poem and was eager to hear responses to it. Gordon commented first: "What I find most interesting here is the strong phallic imagery." Others nodded and wondered aloud whether the references to "poles" and "shafts" should be so blatant, whether I was overplaying the machismo. I listened to these responses with growing discomfort. I was completely unaware of these images but upon rereading the poem had to admit they were there. The group had naturally appropriated the poem as its own, and I had to reckon with their observations, incorporating them into my own renewed perceptions about this poem that seemed to have a mind of its own.

The writer reading to a receptive audience relinquishes some control, while the group gains some power—and a measure of responsibility. I want to bring this principle into classroom workshop sessions as well. I want my students to believe that submitting work for the comments of others carries with it the responsibility of providing something the writer is committed to. At the same time, in its role as collective respondent, critic, editor, and audience, the group is obligated to be honest and thorough. It must exercise some ownership responsibilities.

On occasion, exerting ownership is a real challenge: in the writer's group, if a story, poem, or essay knocks our socks off, all we can say is "Wow!" This doesn't happen often—maybe once a year. Chris Schreiner did it with "Hobby Deep in Hudson Bay," a story he read to us at the first meeting he attended. He brought with him a voice we had never heard before and a cast of crazies out of the Canadian wilderness—which he had never visited. And it happened when Judith Hiott announced she had begun translating Ovid's *Amores* and read to us,

> *Every lover's a soldier; Cupid's troops never dodder.*
> *Believe me, Atticus, every lover is cannon fodder.*
> *The green age for war agrees*
> *also with love: fighting geezers*
> *are vile; randy wheezers are treason.*
> *The want of seasons*
> *Leaders seek in bold soldiers handsome girls*
> *hold dear drafting churls*
> *for their flanks. Both lovers and soldiers keep*
> *vigil by night. The ground's where both sleep,*
> *one by his sweetie's door, one by the general's.*

She went on for several pages, and we were transfixed. We had quibbles, but not many, and Judith's efforts went down in the annals of our writing group not only as the first translation but also as one of the few poems we were unanimously willing to swallow whole.

When my class struggles to formulate a response to a student paper or when one supportive soul says, "I wouldn't change a word!" I seldom agree, but I try at those moments to recall occasions when our writer's group has been handed a little work of art on a platter and has wished only for the luxury of savoring it.

When my classes function as a writer's group, I most relish the times when responses to a draft lead to measurably improved writing—and when the class can see for itself this gratifying end product. A student named Billy once brought in a humdrum draft that began,

> *After my graduation from high school, I decided to attend college, because all my friends were doing so. I thought that college was simply the next step in a normal life, not really understanding the purpose behind continuing my education.*

Yawn. One question we have learned to ask in class about a draft is, "When does our interest really kick in?" (if it ever does). We were nearly a page into Billy's narrative before he began to tell about a summer job his father surprised him with. When a classmate suggested, "Why not surprise us in the same way you were surprised?" I knew I could not have given better advice. Later, his opening paragraph read,

> *When my freshman year in college ended, I drove home dreaming about good food and a summer full of fun. These dreams were shattered the minute I walked in the door. My mother handed me a cold ham sandwich, and my father said, "Son, are you ready to work?"*

An even more dramatic change of direction came in a student's essay about paintball, a militaristic game in which teams of well-armed weekend warriors stalk one another with guns that shoot paint capsules instead of real bullets. The assignment was to do a sort of feature article on some new phenomenon, form of recreation, or popular trend. Tracy's enthusiasm for paintball extended to playing the game himself one Saturday, and he came in with an informative piece that began this way:

> *The sport has been called the ultimate game, gotcha, survivor, capture the flag, and paintball. In America some three million people are regular players and over five thousand new players step onto a field for the first time each week. But just where did this phenomenon come from?*

Students in our class complimented him on the opening sentence and the startling statistics in the second sentence. Few of us had ever heard of this new pastime. But the sudden question in sentence four left us cold, and we agreed that we weren't yet interested enough to wonder about the sport's origins. It needed something. Then one student came up with what in retrospect seem obvious questions: What's it like to be out there playing? Is it play or is it war? Or something in between? If I were the sole respondent to this draft, I'm not sure I would have thought to ask those questions. Class members challenged him to bring us the experience of paintball, not just a string of statistics. Here's the revised opening:

> The remnants of what was once Alpha team gathered on the ridge east of the valley. They had taken five casualties in the last skirmish, a heavy blow to the twelve-man team, but rumors speculated that the opposition was down just as many. They took a defensive position facing the downslope to give the ammo that extra foot or two of range that could be crucial to their survival. As they settled in to wait, they heard the crackling of guns to the sharp right. Before the team commander could take cover, he felt a blistering sting on his back. He reached his hand around to feel where he had been shot. When he brought it back it was colored red. He had been eliminated.
>
> An excerpt from a World War II novel? A Vietnam flashback? Your grandfather's favorite Korean war story? Not really. It's paintball.

I'm delighted with all student writing that—like Tracy's—is unquestionably improved following class response, just as I feel some pride when a poem or story from our writer's group is published. But as important as these specific gains are, the real value of bringing the writer's group into the classroom is what this conveys about writing as a social act. Writing is both the loneliest and the most communal of endeavors. Linda Brodkey challenges us to renounce the lonely garret as the prototypical "scene" of writing and instead to envision writing in the context of a community. And Ann Ruggles Gere, in *Writing Groups: History, Theory, and Implications*, reminds us that writing groups have a long and distinguished history dating from well back into the nineteenth century.

As I make my students a part of this history, I want them to discover the pleasures of going public in private—of reading aloud to and hearing responses from a group of committed writers. I want them to see that the solitude of individual effort is balanced by the voices of others in this conversation that engages all of us—students and teachers alike.

WORKS CITED

Brodkey, Linda. "Modernism and the Scene(s) of Writing." *College English* 49 (1987): 396–418.

Gere, Ann Ruggles. *Writing Groups: History, Theory, and Implications.* Carbondale, IL: Southern Illinois UP, 1987.

I wish to thank Mike Taylor and Judith Hiott from our writer's group, as well as Billy Seals and Tracy Squires from my classes, for providing useful examples.

9

Confessions of
a Failed Bookmaker

STEPHEN TCHUDI

Stephen Tchudi is Professor of English at the University of Nevada, Reno, where he teaches in the rhetoric/composition program. He is the author of thirty books, which range from texts such as the highly acclaimed **Writing in Reality,** *co-authored with James Miller, to nonfiction and fiction books for young adults such as* **The Young Writer's Handbook** *(with Susan Tchudi),* **The Burg-O-Rama Man,** *and* **The Green Machine and the Frog Crusade.** *He is past president of the National Council of Teachers of English and former editor of* **The English Journal.**

I began to write fiction and nonfiction for young adults about ten years ago. Since then I have received invitations to a number of young author conferences, where kids who have written and bound a book gather to share their writing and to be honored as writers. There I have opportunities to talk about how I changed from being a nonwriter to one who likes to begin his day at the typewriter.

I sincerely congratulate the young authors on writing their own books. I then confess that when I was their age I had ambitions to write books but seemed always to fall short. As a kid, I was a failed bookmaker.

I can recall as a first grader starting, but never completing, a "cowboy book" that was to be called *Joe Comes to America.* I remember as a fifth grader planning to co-author a book on magic with my friend Donnie but never getting beyond writing up the first couple of illusions. As a seventh grader, I started one of my own Hardy Boys mysteries, but alas, I never got beyond chapter one. I tell young authors that if I'd had a teacher like theirs, perhaps I would have finished at least one of those books!

Sad to say, those unfinished books were actually the high point of my noncareer as a young writer. By the time I reached eighth grade, I became snared in what I call the Academic Loop, and that restrained my impulses toward writing. Secondary school teachers occasionally offered writing assignments in imaginative discourse modes, but these were often quite restricted in form and content: "Write a sonnet. Shakespearean. Due Tuesday." Most of the writing I did in the college preparatory track at my high school was pseudoacademic in focus, a routine of book reports, study questions, and the traditional senior year research paper.

I occasionally wrote on my own during my high school years, documents for use in the Boy Scouts or church youth fellowship. Once, spontaneously, my buddies and I created a satirical edition of our high school's newspaper, which we circulated privately among friends and teachers whom we knew would appreciate it. I think such self-sponsored writing may have helped to preserve my natural style despite the demands of the Academic Loop. Still, I finished high school feeling quite uncertain about my skills as a writer.

Once in college, my writing life became downright grim. In what appears to me to have been a Rite of Passage, the freshman writing course was based on a pedagogical device called the "Yes/ No" theme. Every freshman in the college wrote impromptu essays each Friday on topics selected from the week's reading— the text was the Old Testament of *The Bible*. Our instructors gave us one of two grades for these impromptus: "Yes" if the theme was perfect; "No" if it contained a single error of usage, mechanics, or spelling. We had to get two "Yes" themes out of twelve to pass the course.

The "Yes/No" themes influenced my writing powerfully. Aside from scaring me (and the rest of the freshman class) half to death, they drove out what little imagination and spark was left in my writing. The trick to writing "perfect" themes was to use simple words that one knew how to spell, to use short sentences that couldn't become fouled by complicated syntax, and to be absolutely conventional in structure: state the thesis, number the reasons, sum up at the close. This was bread-and-butter, plain-style Academic Loop writing of the most mechanical sort.

Although the freshman comp course was destructive to what we now call "personal voice," I believe that a writing impulse survived in me, the impulse that had led me to start the Cowboy Joe and magic and Hardy boys books, that had led to the high school newspaper satire. However, it wasn't until I was well out of the Academic Loop, several years beyond graduate school, that I got into serious bookmaking. Ironically, this came about as a byproduct of editing a professional academic journal.

As editor of *The English Journal* from 1973 to 1980, I wrote a monthly "Editor's Page." At first I focused these columns on an overview of the month's content. Eventually, however, I became bored with this standard expository prose and began inserting a bit more of my own personality. One time I wrote a mild diatribe called "Who Resurrected Bonehead English?" in protest to the then (and now) faddish practice of making fun of the writing gaffes of first-year students. Another time I did a bit of editorializing on "Why Journalists Can't Teach," objecting to media articles that offered a quick fix to the writing "crisis." I wrote a fantasy, "I Met Johnny and Jane," in which I imagined the future of education depending on whether back-to-basics or student-centered views of education won out. And I did some satire: a Thurberesque piece called "A Likely Story" in which it is revealed that the writing crisis was created by the telephone industry as a way of promoting long distance calls.

Nobody complained about the more imaginative of my editorials. In fact, readers seemed to like them, to welcome them as an alternative. I didn't get fired from my university position, and above all, I found this stuff fun to write.

From that seven-year experience of writing editorials—sixty-three in all—my range and breadth as a writer was considerably extended. When I finished my stint as editor, I found my own writing moving in new directions. In particular, I ventured into writing for young people, where, I've discovered, editors and publishers seem more open to new directions and experiments than are the editors of books for adults.

I've found that just about anything you're interested in can find its way into a book. What began as my hobby of making root beer at home led to a history of soft drinks (*Soda Poppery*). My interest in writing generated a nonfiction book for kids (*The Young Writer's Handbook*), and my fascination with learning led to another (*The Young Learner's Handbook*). I've long been intrigued by how people go about explaining mysteries to themselves, so I have just published *Probing the Unknown,* a book that also got me back into writing about magic. I also turned to fiction, where I mined past experience. Frustrations with high school football coaches turned up as chapters in *The Burg-O-Rama Man,* and a childhood hobby of collecting frogs provided the starting point for *The Green Machine and the Frog Crusade.*

I like to tell my writing autobiography to young writers (and anybody else who will listen to or read it), because it helps to emphasize one of the most important of my learnings about writing: that *anyone* can be a writer. Each of us has a mind filled with ideas and experiences that can be gotten down on paper. I'm absolutely convinced that the major difference between writers and nonwriters is simply that the writers have the confidence, opportunity, and support to write regularly.

I emphasize, too, that as people extend their experience, their language skills are extended and stretched as well. That observation is not original with me, of course. It is a paraphrase of the central thesis of John Dixon's book *Growth through English* (National Association for the Teaching of English and National Council of Teachers of English, 1968, 1976). Dixon is correct when he says that *experience* drives language, that if you have ideas and a desire to express them, you'll find the necessary language. For example, I was surprised to find myself publishing a *novel* at the age of forty. I had no training as a writer of fiction, merely a background as a reader and as a writer of nonfiction. When I began my novel, however, I found that the story I had to tell—*The Burg-O-Rama Man*—pretty much found its own structure and language, though not without a great deal of hard work.

However, I've also learned that ideas often expand to fill writing opportunities, so I actively seek out new audiences and forms to explore. I never say "no" to an invitation to write. As a concrete example: A theater group in California expressed an interest in doing *The Burg-O-Rama Man* as a play. I hadn't written any drama since I'd done a skit for Boy Scouts. Although the California group said they'd be willing to write the adaptation, I decided I'd rather take a shot at it myself. In writing the script I learned a great deal about play writing and production and about my own writing processes and interests. I even discovered and explored the novel anew. My writing skills and understandings grew in response to the opportunity to write. Thus, although

I remain committed to the "growth through English" view and emphasize to novice writers that their own experiences are more important than the vagaries of "writing skill," I also think they need nudging to find new avenues and outlets for their composing.

Writing in various forms and genres has also changed my view of the relationship between so-called *imaginative* or *creative* writing and nonfiction or *expository* writing. The two should not—*cannot*—be separated. Many people seem to feel they involve two distinct sets of skills. Indeed, a great many people in the Academic Loop distrust creative writing because they think it is ephemeral, effusive, and unduly "expressive." Teachers generally acknowledge the value of creative writing (especially if done by the English and American masters), but they worry that poetry, prose, or drama invites young writers to be disorganized and to write on whim or "inspiration."

To the contrary, I find that imaginative writing requires even more structure than exposition. In a novel, poem, or play, there is no room for unclear organization or imprecise language. Ironically, I now see exposition as tolerating *less* precise structuring than imaginative writing. In an essay, after all, you can always use topic sentences, transitions, restatements, summaries, conclusions, and the like to make your meaning explicit. No such devices are available to the imaginative writer, who must necessarily "show, not tell."

Learning about that relationship has led me to conclude that even in the Academic Loop, it's okay to employ imaginative elements in exposition: to put a little jelly on your bread-and-butter writing. My nonfiction prose style has been greatly aided by my ventures into imaginative writing. I've discovered that I don't always have to write my "bread-and-butter" papers with the same seriousness and plainness as my old Yes/No themes.

Perhaps the most important thing I have learned from my writing autobiography is that writers must discover their own truths—both what they want to write and how they go about getting writing done. I hope that my story is helpful and encouraging to writers of all ages, but I am very cautious about saying "Do it this way." One of the great weaknesses in our teaching system, I think, is that we are often unwilling to take the idea of "learning by doing" seriously. In a well meaning effort to help our students, we offer them generalizations rather than experience. For instance, the idea of writing-as-process seems, these days, dangerously close to being reduced to a formula for all children to follow.

As a writing teacher who writes, I see my most important task as convincing students to accept the validity of their own experience. I may have failed as a young bookmaker, but I'm now persuaded, both by my own experience and by meeting with the new breed of young authors, that every one of us has books and books inside us just waiting to be written.

10

What Helen Gurley Brown Taught Me about Teaching Basic Writing

SUSAN OSBORN

Susan Osborn's first novel, **Surviving the Wreck,** *for which she received a New Jersey State Arts Council fellowship for 1989/90, will be published by Henry Holt in 1991. Her reviews, essays, and articles have appeared in* **The Village Voice, The American Book Review, Newsday, The Philadelphia Inquirer, The Chicago Sun-Times,** *and* **The 60's Without Apology** *ed. by Stanley Aronowitz et al, among others. Before turning her attention to fiction, Ms. Osborn completed thirteen books of nonfiction. She also teaches composition and gender studies at Rutgers University.*

At age twenty-two, broke and suffering the confidence only the very poor and the very romantic can suffer, I moved to Manhattan, certain that my pockets would soon be swelled by the weight of literary success. Despite my swagger, I admit I was totally unprepared for my first assignment, offered by one of Helen Gurley Brown's editors at *Cosmo*. Swallowing hard, I listened as she suggested the possibilities for freelance articles to me: "How I Survived My Husband's Infidelity," "A Crash Course

in Foreign Affairs," and "Revenge: Naughty, But Oh So Satisfying."

"Well?" she whispered as if she had just offered me something
from a trolley of sweets.

"Haven't you really got anything a bit more literary?" I asked,
clipping the t's hard and skipping the second syllable in "literary"
in the hopes that a demonstration of my newly acquired British
ancestry might compel a recognition of my true literary talents.

Swiveling her chair away from me, she pulled hard on a straw
sticking out from her can of diet Coke and chided, "What *are*
you doing in New York?"

"Well," I began impressively, my mouth as dry as a rice cake,
"I just moved here with my boyfriend..."

"How to Handle the Brand New Lover in Your or His Bed!"
she announced gleaming. She shot a scented sheet of paper
decorated with Helen Gurley Brown's flowery notes from across
her desk.

"I want this one outrageous," the Editor-in-Chief had written.
"Aim for the rogue-types, the lady desperados... You know who
I'm talking about... *You're the expert here*... Use what you know;
this one shouldn't be researched. *Rely on your own ideas, your own
experience...*"

I looked up at the editor who was working the straw with her
teeth.

This is simply impossible, I thought. After all, I may have been
broke, but I was a college graduate; this was not, I was sure,
what my parents had expected from me.

"I'll take it," I said, trying to work my lips into some semblance
of a smile.

Now what was I to do? There were no reference books, no
research libraries to help. In high school and college I was never
my own expert. "Four footnotes to every page" was the rule for
flat summaries I wrote in ninth grade. Wanting to cultivate gold-
star status, I tripled that in college, compelling my instructors
to hire a small U-Haul everytime I submitted a paper. Only once
did I read: "Excellent resume of Che's thinking.... However, I
would have liked to hear more about *your* ideas on the New
Socialist Man...." I blamed this inexplicable request on the professor's burgeoning alcoholism and continued to hide my responses behind a summary of the ideas of "experts."

But this *Cosmo* assignment forced me to interpret a text (all
right, perhaps that is a slightly euphemistic term for some of the

"texts" I explored before marriage) and to find a way of writing without hiding behind the ideas of experts. There was no way I could approach this assignment in the traditional academic way. *"You're the expert,"* Helen Gurley Brown had written. I was forced, for the first time, to use my ideas and my experience. The assignment challenged me to take responsibility for defining my subject, to make decisions about significance, utility, and authority (should I write about the time I entertained the Yalie after the last boozy dorm party, or perhaps I'd make my point more effectively with one of my first New York trysts?) and to develop a specialized vocabulary to describe those concepts (do I call the first hour Temptation Time? And the last, Better Luck Next Time?). And I had to define my own voice—for the first time—not ape the objective, scholarly tone of my academic forebears. For the first time in my life, then, I wasn't just copying somebody else's ideas but was actually composing, inventing myself as a writer. In other words, I had, for the first time, actively implicated myself in the construction of meaning.

In a way, this assignment engaged me as no previous writing assignment had. Admittedly, I began hesitantly and formed only a tenuous relationship with the material before me, but I ended with an enormous swell of confidence that came not of mastery necessarily, but of having taken risks and of having authorized my own response. It was the beginning of my transformation from scribe to writer.

Shortly after my *Cosmo* assignment, I landed a position as the Feature Writer for the Hearst's newly inaugurated *Country Living* magazine. Within a year, I had left *Country Living* and was writing trade books on a variety of subjects, including antiques, collectibles, health issues, and fashion; I did interviews, profiles, and book reviews for nationally circulated newspapers and small journals; I wrote jacket blurbs, press releases, book proposals, and flap copy; I even managed to squeeze in some time for fiction. However, my swift success was, paradoxically, hard on the ego.

As a white, bright, middle-class kid, I had been nursed on the myth of genius, rocked in the cradle of specialness. The ability to write well, I had been taught, is a natural gift. Writing was not, in other words, a matter of exercising rhetorical options and developing strategies for use in different situations; it was not about negotiating meaning in a constantly shifting dialogue between reader, writer, and text. Rather, it was an inherent ability one had or didn't have, and I had been encouraged to believe myself one of the chosen.

But my experience as a paid, professional writer contradicted this theory. Writing seemed to have less to do with natural gifts than with conscious and deliberate hard work, and I came to conceive of myself more as a laborer than a muse-inspired poet. And people began talking to me about writing in a way that my teachers never had. Suddenly, editors were talking about "voice" and "audience." Nobody said a word about rules for punctuation and style; those matters, it seemed, were taken care of later, after the real work was done, by people called copy editors. I learned by experimenting. For example, one of my first assignments was to write a book on American rustic furniture. During my research, I became fascinated by the story of an early Adirondack explorer. I went after his story with graduate student zeal and presented my editor with a six-thousand word analysis of the explorer's failed philosophy of the wilderness, poorly disguised as an introductory chapter. My editor was kind: "Our book is not for scholars, dear, but Yuppies. Think of your audience. Be kind to them, won't you, and modify the voice somewhat?" Out went the polysyllabic prose, the dovetailed sentences, the dry, erudite analysis, and in its place was inserted a much shorter introduction written in a cheerful, even facile, voice that was far more appropriate to the assignment. I was also encouraged, as I had been for my *Cosmo* assignment, to use my own experience. "Have you ever sat in a chair made of sticks and twigs," my editor asked. "Well, just what does it feel like?"

Each day, I made conscious, strategic choices about voice, content, and structure, which varied with each assignment. For example, in the morning I might work on a fashion book and write in a vivacious voice that I thought would appeal to my readers and in the afternoon, switch to book reviews in which my voice became sober, at times witty or ironical. Each time, the choice was a strategic one, based on my knowledge of my audience, my assignment, and my own needs as a writer. My professional writing was not, therefore, random or muse-dependent, nor did it seem something I was uniquely, genetically inclined to, but deliberate and meaningful behavior that I could control and manipulate according to the situational context.

My descent from the pantheon of the select few was, momentarily, deflating; however, as frequently happens, my financial remuneration quickly overcame my bruised pride, and I thought no more about it until I approached my first remedial writing classroom, a job I assumed as a favor to a friend who was, due to illness, unable to teach one term.

I admit, I was unprepared. I had learned from my liberal minded mentors that BWs must be handled with care (lest we be accused of being mean?) and that they mustn't be pushed too hard or too far (because of their "handicaps"?). Teaching basic writing was not, they said, about helping students exercise rhetorical options and encouraging the development of strategies for negotiating meaning; it was about beating them over the head with rules that had little to do with real writing situations.

What was one to do? (Some might ask, why bother teaching at all?) Tucking a copy of *Harbrace* beneath my arm, I marched forward.

Four months later, I was thrust out again, this time by the students who, having mastered *Harbrace*'s rules (which they could, to my chagrin, recite from memory) but receiving only C's for the course (the meager extent of my largesse), somehow managed not to throttle me. It was clear: something had gone terribly wrong.

Despite my frustration, I continued to teach (regular paychecks, regardless of how meagre, are at times irresistible to the freelancer), but the next semester I turned not to *Harbrace* but to the students. I began listening more attentively to their explanations. For example, one student began an essay with the following sentence: "Eating at Burger King is always a palatable experience." When I asked him to explain what he meant by "palatable," he explained, "That's a word I thought you would like." When I pressed further, he said, "You know, it's the kind of word you use in school." Another student made the following changes in the beginning of her essay:

> *Burger King food appeals to people in many different ways, but as a whole, it is of little nutritional value. It isn't h ... Unfortunately, it isn't healthy to eat.*

When I asked her why she had changed the sentence, she explained that she wanted a "more personal sounding essay" and cited her change from the clinical sounding "nutritional value" to the more conversational "healthy." She also said she had made the change because "You seemed like somebody who'd like it less stuffy."

In other words, what both these writers were saying to me is that they had, like any good writer, made conscious and deliberate choices about voice and diction based on their knowledge of the assignment, the audience, and their own personal intention. Although they didn't use the words "voice" and "audience," their textual changes and choices reflected their concern with these issues. In other words, what I learned was that their concerns as writers were really not any different from mine.

As my third semester approached, I sought to develop pedagogical strategies that were not "remedial" or "developmental" per se but rather strategies that would create a classroom situation in which students might recognize writing not as a rule- or formula-bound activity but as a matter of options and choices that can be exercised depending on the requirements of particular writing situations. I wanted to move away from instruction that deauthorized BWs (and made them feel even more like dummies) and toward one that encouraged students' active implication in the construction of meaning. As Helen Gurley Brown might put it, I wanted them to be the experts, not me.

My goals, then, were twofold. First, I wanted to create a classroom situation in which the apparent gap between me and them might be bridged and to find ways of dramatizing to them their own deliberate, conscious, and ongoing writerly processes. Second, I wanted them to feel and act like experts, not amateurs approximating "real" writing behavior.

I now don't teach BWs any differently than honors students—and I don't treat them any differently than I do professional writers. I don't coddle them, nor do I try to beat them into submission; rather, I treat them as professionals with a job to do. We talk, not in terms of rules but in terms of audience, voice, assignment, and personal intention. They don't write summaries of other peoples' ideas, nor do we spend time mining for other writers' "main" points. Rules of usage or style are only discussed when they pertain to a specific concern in a student's essay.

We now begin the semester not with *Harbrace* but with a brainstorming session. During the course of the semester, we talk about the difference between writing a letter to a parent, a friend, a lover, or a spouse. We read essays written by different writers holding the same view about an issue and analyze the difference in voice between the two essays. As a follow-up to this exercise, we discuss the appropriateness of various voices for various audiences. I also ask students to analyze the voice in

seven different writing samples of mine and ask them to speculate about the kind of audience for whom I was writing. The
astuteness of their commentary frequently astounds me; it reflects their ability to understand writing as a process involving
negotiation and strategizing. As a follow-up to this exercise, I
ask them to submit different samples of their own writing (a
letter to a child, a memo to a boss, a note left for a friend) for
analysis, and we discuss possible reasons the writer adopted the
strategies he or she did, based on our knowledge of the assignment and audience.

As important, I ask students, as Helen Gurley Brown asked
me, to use their own experience, to be their own experts. As did
I, they begin hesitantly and form only a cautious relationship
with the material before them, but most end the semester with
a rush of confidence that comes not of mastery necessarily but
of having taken risks and authorized their own responses.

11

Writing and Responding

MICHAEL ROBERTSON

Michael Robertson, after graduating from Stanford University, worked as a freelance journalist in New York, where he published articles and reviews on dance, theater, and film in **Dance Magazine, The Village Voice, The New York Times,** *and other publications. He did graduate work at Princeton University and served for three years as Director of Princeton's freshman composition course. Currently Assistant Professor of English at Lafayette College, where he also teaches in the American Civilization program, he is writing a book on Stephen Crane's journalism.*

I learned to write—I mean really learned something about how best to send a message I cared about to a largely anonymous audience—when I was in my twenties, had completed four years of college, and was trying to make a living as a freelance journalist and critic. My belated instruction came courtesy of an editor at a magazine that I wrote for regularly. Her lessons did not take place in a classroom—did not even take place in person—and consisted solely of detailed responses to my writing. Occasionally now, when I'm racking my brain to come up with an innovative lesson plan, I think of my editor's lessons and acknowledge that what I do in a classroom may be less important to my students than what I tell them about the essay that they've just turned in. In other words, the universally dreaded task of responding to a stack of student papers may be our best opportunity for teaching.

The teacher whose comments on my writing now serve as a model for my own responses to students was an editor at *Dance Magazine* whom I'll call Rachel. In what I now recognize as a gesture of blind faith, Rachel had hired me to write a monthly column of reviews. At the time, I had been living in New York City for a couple of years. Caught up in the excitement of the New York theater and dance scene, my wife and I had been attending plays and dance performances several nights a week. Gradually, as I became more knowledgeable about what I was seeing, I began writing reviews and features for some New York City weeklies. After a few months of this, I decided to take a long shot and sent a couple of sample reviews to *Dance Magazine,* a national magazine edited in New York. Soon afterwards, I got a call from Rachel. To my surprise, she put my name on the masthead, assigned me some performances to review, and told me not to miss my deadline. Suddenly, I was a dance critic.

The problem was that not only did I have little experience writing dance criticism, but in four years of college I had learned little about writing in general. As an English major, I had dutifully turned in dozens of essays. My teachers had dutifully graded and returned them. But during all those years of grades and brief comments—"Good work" or "Your interpretation of the poem isn't fully developed"—no one had ever asked me to revise a paper or told me anything about how I might approach the next essay differently. No one, that is, had taught me how a writer works.

Since *Dance Magazine* is a monthly, the deadline pressure was not as intense as at the weekly magazines that I'd written for previously. Rachel, a naturally gifted teacher, had time to instruct me in the craft of writing. Every month, I would type my reviews on the magazine's special narrow-column paper with numbered lines and turn them in to Rachel. The next day I'd get a phone call from her. "Do you have your copy with you?" she'd begin. "Okay, let's start with page one, line twelve: Doesn't this sentence contradict what you said about the performance in your opening?" And so it would go, page by page, line by line, with Rachel asking one question after another. She never rewrote anything for me, never even altered a comma. Mostly, she just asked questions. Sometimes she questioned my use of a semicolon, but she was just as likely to ask about the principles behind what I'd said. "Page twelve, line seven: you say that the dance should be shortened. Do you really think that it's a critic's task to advise an artist how to alter her work?" While we talked,

I scribbled notes. The following day I would deliver my revised article to the magazine.

Though Rachel was a good teacher, I can't claim to have been a particularly quick student. But over the course of the three years that I wrote for the magazine, my monthly conversations with her gradually became briefer. She had fewer questions to ask about what I had written, and her queries more often dealt with specific issues of style or content rather than with basic approaches to writing criticism. In short, I was becoming a better writer, able to anticipate the questions that Rachel—or any reader—might have.

I eventually left New York City and freelance journalism in order to go to graduate school. Like most English graduate students, I soon found myself teaching freshman composition. And like most beginning teachers, I discovered that one of the most difficult parts of the job was figuring out how to respond to my students' writing. For me, the dilemma was choosing between different models of response. On the one hand, it was easy to fall into the pattern set by my college and graduate school teachers: responding to student essays by simply writing a grade, some marginal comments, and a brief endnote. On the other hand, my experience with Rachel suggested a different way of teaching students to write. If I followed Rachel's methods, my comments on students' completed essays were largely irrelevant. The time to respond was while essays were still in draft, and my response should consist mostly of questions aimed at helping students to revise.

During my first semesters of teaching, I began reading articles and books about the process theory of teaching composition. It didn't take long to figure out that my English professors followed what has been called the "current-traditional" paradigm of teaching writing, paying attention only to the written product. Rachel, I realized, instinctively held to a newer paradigm that focuses on the process by which writers arrive at a final product. To use Donald Murray's metaphors, my English professors saw their role as that of judge, evaluating students' completed essays. Rachel was not judge but physician, diagnosing what ailed the drafts of my articles and prescribing measures for improving them.[1]

Over time, I began modeling my teaching more and more on

[1]Donald Murray, *A Writer Teaches Writing* (Boston: Houghton Mifflin, 1968) 19.

Rachel's example. I tried to abstract the principles that made her responses to me so helpful and use them in my own comments on student writing. Later, when I became director of a university composition program, I started to teach those principles to novice instructors and came up with four basic guidelines for responding.

MOST COMMENTS SHOULD BE AIMED AT REVISION

When I first began teaching, I spent lots of time writing extensive comments on my students' finished papers. I thought this was part of being a conscientious teacher, even though I often watched in dismay as students glanced at their grade and ignored all my carefully crafted remarks.

Now I follow Rachel's model. As a professional editor, Rachel responded only to writers' drafts; once an article was completed, she considered her work done. I try to bring some of the same professionalism into the classroom. I now write only a brief comment on a student's final paper; all that's needed is to explain the reasoning behind the grade. My detailed response appears on work–in–progress, when I know students won't ignore my remarks in favor of the "real" message of a grade.

I try to remember, though, that shifting most of my commentary to drafts doesn't automatically mean that my responses will be helpful. I've benefited a lot from Nancy Sommers's cautionary tale in her article "Responding to Student Writing," which reports on her study of college teachers' comments on students' drafts.[2] She found that the instructors' responses—supposedly written to encourage revision—were frequently contradictory; teachers would tell students to make major revisions by adding, deleting, or reorganizing information, while at the same time giving suggestions for editing individual sentences. The sentence-level comments were at best wasted effort, since any individual sentence was likely either to disappear or to be significantly altered as students revised. At worst, the contradictory comments prompted students to concentrate on fixing easily correctable stylistic problems while ignoring more significant issues such as content and organization. Sommers's article serves

[2]Nancy Sommers, "Responding to Student Writing," *College Composition and Communication* 33 (1982): 148–56.

as a useful reminder that comments should help students to understand revision as a genuine re-seeing of what they have on paper, not just as a process of getting the commas right.

RESPOND TO CONTENT

While she was attentive to the style of my writing, Rachel's main focus was on what I had said. Were my points clear? Had I adequately defended my judgments? Like music, dance is a notoriously difficult art to describe, and Rachel was ruthless in pointing out instances where I had failed to give a clear picture of what the movement on stage looked like.

As a professional writer, I took for granted Rachel's focus on the content of my articles. Several years later, as a composition program director reviewing instructors' comments on student papers, I was struck by how common it is for teachers to ignore what students say and to comment exclusively on how they say it. Nancy Sommers reported that the teachers in her study gave so little attention to content that the comments on any paper could have been rubber-stamped onto any other.

Good writing depends in part on the writer's desire to communicate a message. When teachers respond only to an essay's form—no matter whether to lower level stylistic concerns or to major issues of organization—students are left to assume that we don't take their message seriously. Writers who get nothing but criticism of their errors are likely to view writing as a journey through a minefield of potential errors; they may well conclude that the best way to prevent making frequent mistakes is to avoid writing as much as possible once they leave our classes. Even writers who receive positive comments about form—such as "good introduction," "effective transition," "strong conclusion"—may come to regard writing, at least, classroom writing, as a mechanical process of following the rules, not as a means of communicating a message they care about.

When I began leading workshops for writing teachers, I found that some instructors who agreed in principle with my arguments for responding to the content of students' essays were nevertheless reluctant to do so. Often, they mentioned the difficulty of responding to essays on controversial issues such as abortion, capital punishment, feminism, or race relations. On the one hand, they pointed out, students may try to guess the teacher's opinion in order to be rewarded for promoting the "right" view; on the other, students may view a teacher's negative response to content as punishment for being on the "wrong" side.

I agree that we have to be careful in responding to provocative or controversial essays, but I don't think we have to abandon attention to content. One solution is to adopt a persona. For example, I've taken on the identity of a poor, unmarried teenage mother to respond to student essays on abortion. Once I used the voice of Martin Luther King, Jr. in "Letter from a Birmingham Jail"—an essay we'd studied in class—to respond to a student who wrote about race. But it's not necessary to adopt a formal persona in order to respond to a controversial topic without imposing an opinion on students. Comments that raise questions and suggest how various readers might react to an essay provide a way to talk about content and point out shortcomings in a student's argument while still demonstrating respect for students' right to their own views.[3]

ESTABLISH A DIALOGUE

Rachel's monthly telephone conversations were superb opportunities for teaching and learning. She could raise questions about my intended meaning, and I had the chance to respond immediately or to note problem areas and rewrite them later. Though the composition classes at my college are alarmingly large, I try to follow Rachel's model by holding individual conferences with each student several times during the semester. These conferences are an invaluable means of establishing a dialogue, of making sure that students have the major say in determining how to revise their writing.[4] Of course, holding a conference does not guarantee that real dialogue will take place; I know how easy it is to transform a conference into a monologue in which the student's only role is to listen passively to my instructions on how to fix a paper. However, so long as I keep the

[3]I describe other strategies for responding to content in " 'Is Anybody Listening?': Responding to Student Writing," *College Composition and Communication* 37 (1986): 87–91.
[4]Some pioneering instructors use conferences as their sole means of responding to student writing; Roger Garrison and Donald Murray have written influential articles describing entire composition courses based on one-to-one conferences.

emphasis on questioning a writer's choices rather than prescribing solutions, I find conferences one of the best ways to respond to student writing.

I also use a variety of techniques to help establish a dialogue on paper. One simple method is to ask students to turn in a separate page of commentary along with their essay. I ask them to respond to questions: What is your purpose in this essay? What's your favorite part? What part are you unhappy with? And I have them ask me questions in turn. I find that students can often identify perceptively the aspects of their papers that need revision; their questions are often calls for confirmation and suggestions. "Do you think my introduction is dull?" one student recently wrote in her commentary. "Do you have any ideas of how I could grab readers' attention better?" A student doing a paper on teenage drinking asked, "Do I need to add some statistics into my argument? Should I do some research on auto accidents involving teenagers who are drunk?" Comments like these make a teacher's job easy and encourage me to see my role more as friendly adviser confirming students' own ideas about how to revise rather than as draconian enforcer of rules.

When it comes to writing my own response, I follow three self-imposed rules to encourage a sense of dialogue. First, I start by addressing the student by name, and I use first person frequently. It's harder to assume a magisterial tone or to fall into sarcasm when you write a comment in the same style that you'd use in a letter to a friend.

Next, following Rachel's model, I ask a lot of questions. Some questions are repeated frequently: What's your purpose in this paragraph? Why do you say this? Other questions are more specific. For a recent set of papers on America's drug policy, I asked one student, "Aren't there any people who oppose needle-exchange programs for drug addicts?" To another I wrote, "I'm confused by your section on legalization of drugs. Are you saying that one option is to legalize cocaine and heroin but not marijuana?" Obviously, some of my questions are more open-ended than others. But any question can let students know that they have a role to play in this dialogue about meaning; students' responses to queries will determine how they revise their papers.

Last, when I think it's appropriate to give students a direct suggestion for revising, I try to offer alternatives. For example, one of my students writing about drug policy didn't narrow her topic sufficiently. I wrote to her, "You treat both legalizing drugs and emphasizing prevention. That's a lot to cover in a short essay; this could be more effective if you limited yourself to one of those topics in your revision. As it stands, your discussion of prevention is much more specific, but the legalization topic has a lot of potential. Which would you prefer to focus on?" Offering alternatives for revision is another means of ensuring that I don't impose my own ideas on a student; it's a way of demonstrating the significant choices that writers have as they shape their work.

POINT OUT GENERAL PRINCIPLES OF GOOD WRITING

As an editor, Rachel's immediate concern was improving the articles scheduled for next month's issue. But as a natural teacher, she often went beyond making suggestions on how to revise a particular piece and raised general issues about writing, which I could then apply to future articles.

To help ensure that my comments on student papers address larger issues of writing, I read a paper over once before I write anything on it, and I put most of my commentary in an endnote. Reading the entire paper first helps me to avoid overwhelming the student with advice. Putting most of my commentary in an endnote aids me in pointing out to students what issues are most important. When students look at marginal comments, a note about usage may well appear to have the same importance as a remark about logic or structure; putting the bulk of my response in an endnote allows me to set priorities more easily.

I also try to include a recommendation for the student's next essay in all my responses. For example, I might ask a student to write a different type of introduction, to use a more concise style, or to provide more supporting evidence. Of course, if I ask a student to try a particular technique in a future paper, I have to remember what I said so that I can comment on how successful the student was. Rachel, who worked with only a few writers, could keep in mind her previous comments and each person's general progress. For those of us with one or more large composition classes, it's not so easy to remember either a student's work or our own responses. I find it crucial to keep some sort of record. Since I started writing my comments on a computer a few years ago, record keeping has become a simple matter. I set up for each student a computer-file where I save all my responses; each time I write a new comment, I can rapidly review what I've written earlier. Teachers who type their comments can slip in some carbon paper in order to make a record. For teachers who handwrite their comments directly on the paper, it's a simple matter to jot down a brief summary of the response and note any recommendations made for the next paper.

Keeping a record of my comments is useful not only as a means of tracking my students' progress but as a way of monitoring my own methods of response, of noting when I fall into the easy, authoritarian modes of telling students how to revise rather than asking questions and encouraging them to find their own solutions. Occasionally, I find myself asking how Rachel might handle a particularly difficult paper. She continues to serve as a model, reminding me that responding to writing is at the heart of helping students learn to write.

SELECTED BIBLIOGRAPHY

This list contains works on responding to student writing that I have found particularly helpful.

Anson, Chris M., ed. *Writing and Response: Theory, Practice, and Research.* Urbana, IL: NCTE, 1989.

Beaven, Mary H. "Individualized Goal Setting, Self-Evaluation, and Peer Evaluation." *Evaluating Writing: Describing, Measuring, Judging.* Ed. Charles R. Cooper and Lee Odell. Urbana, IL: NCTE, 1977.

Brannon, Lil, and C. H. Knoblauch. "On Students' Rights to Their Own Texts: A Model of Teacher Response." *College Composition and Communication* 33 (1982): 157–66.

Garrison, Roger H. "One-to-One: Tutorial Instruction in Freshman Composition." *New Directions for Community Colleges* 2 (1974): 55–84.

Hairston, Maxine. "On Not Being a Composition Slave." *Training the New Teacher of College Composition.* Ed. Charles W. Bridges. Urbana, IL: NCTE, 1986. 117–24.

Haswell, Richard H. "Minimal Marking." *College English* 45 (1983): 600–04.

Lees, Elaine O. "Evaluating Student Writing." *College Composition and Communication* 30 (1979): 370–74.

Lindemann, Erika. *A Rhetoric for Writing Teachers.* New York: Oxford UP, 1982.

Murray, Donald. "The Listening Eye: Reflections on the Writing Conference." *College English* 41 (1979): 13–18.

———. *A Writer Teaches Writing.* Boston: Houghton Mifflin, 1968.

Sommers, Nancy. "Responding to Student Writing." *College Composition and Communication* 33 (1982): 148–56.

Stanford, Gene, et al., eds. *How to Handle the Paper Load.* Urbana, IL: NCTE, 1979.

12

Taking What You Need, Giving What You Can: The Writer as Student and Teacher

DAVID HUDDLE

David Huddle's books of fiction and poetry are **Stopping by Home, The High Spirits, Only the Little Bone, Paper Boy,** *and* **A Dream with No Stump Roots in It.** *He has held two fellowships from the National Endowment of the Arts and fellowships from Yaddo and the Virginia Center for the Creative Arts. He is a professor of English at the University of Vermont, as well as a regular staff member of the Bread Loaf Writers' Conference and the Bread Loaf School of English. His work has appeared in* **Esquire, Harper's, The New York Times Magazine, Playboy, Ploughshares,** *and* **Virginia Quarterly Review,** *among others.*

The kind of writer and the kind of teacher of writing I am these days is powerfully informed by my experience as a student of writing. As an undergraduate I had four semesters of creative writing, and I completed the work for two different graduate writing programs. Altogether, I studied under eleven different writing teachers. If ever there was a product of the American

Creative Writing Industry, I am it. And yet in the composition of this essay, I have come to realize that I was equipped with an essential quality, without which I never would have become any kind of writer at all: I was able to take what I needed from every teacher and every class, and I was able to disregard what I didn't need or what might have harmed me. I'm not sure what to name this quality—survival aptitude, perhaps—but it seems to me necessary for anyone who aspires to make a writing life for him- or herself. It seems to me the one quality that perhaps you are born with or born without. If you have it—if you can take what you need from your experience to nourish your writing—then you can learn to write, and the classroom will be of enormous benefit to you. If you don't have it, then no amount of writing education will make you a writer.

So I know that writing can be taught, but I also know that only a small number of people can learn to be writers. In my writing classes I encounter many students who have more talent, more writerly resources (e.g., intelligence, language aptitude, literary instinct) than I have ever had, but who do not become writers. I also encounter a few students whose talents and resources are modest but who nevertheless become writers. In the past I have been frustrated by such unlikely results of my classes. Nowadays I am comforted by that unpredictable element of teaching writing.

In composing this essay and discussing it with my writer-friends, I've come to see that just as a real writer takes what he or she needs from a teacher, so, too, does a writing teacher give what he or she can. It is not my duty to tailor my teaching to each individual student; it is not my duty to attempt to make writers of my students. It is my duty to be a certain kind of a teacher, to try to be consistent in the values that I try to convey to my students, and to let them use me as they will—as I used my teachers.

My relationship with writing and with literature is a practical one. I was years coming to understand this relationship, and in the process, I flunked out of the University of Virginia as an English major. In 1962 and 1963, I knew that I was powerfully affected by many of the novels, stories, and poems I was reading for my classes, but I couldn't get the hang of writing papers, saying the right things in class, or *thinking about literature* in the way that apparently my professors thought about it. Not only that, some of the lectures and discussions from those classes seemed to me deeply wrong but in a way that I couldn't even approach articulating.

I remember three different occasions of English major stall-out—trying to write papers on Salinger's *Nine Stories,* Conrad's *Nostromo,* and Melville's *Moby Dick.* These were books that I deeply loved. I wasn't able to make myself write those papers because (I later understood) I couldn't connect what I felt about the books with the way—the conventional way—I thought the papers had to be written. This wasn't really the fault of my literature professors; if I had been able to think of an alternative and personally meaningful way for me to write the papers, my instructors most likely would have accommodated me, perhaps even rewarded me for being innovative. But at the age of twenty, I didn't have enough gumption to invent my own alternative methods.

What's the difference between academic and practical approaches to narrative literature? Thematic concerns, symbolism, literary history, and matters of influence were, in those days, the stuff of the academic approach to literature. A practical-minded reader would be drawn to such elements as characterization, situation, point of view, structure, setting, pacing, symmetry, diction, syntax, and sentence length. An academic teacher is— or was in those days—interested in the ultimate value of a literary work and its connection to other literary works; a writing teacher is interested in how a work works and does not work.

I'm still reacting to those academically inclined professors. *Workshop* is the word that I put forth in opposition to whatever I see as academic. I'm a committed workshop teacher. I see my job as one of constantly trying to demonstrate to my students the value of a practical approach, not only to manuscripts that pass through our classrooms, but also to works of literature. I want the writing workshop to be a place where it is all right to love *The Sound and the Fury* for entirely different reasons than those that make it attractive to professors and A-plus students of Modern American Literature.

As part of the practical approach to literature, I want my students to see that most aspects of a literary work are down-to-earth matters that are perfectly understandable to a moderately intelligent reader using common sense. Throughout my high school and undergraduate education I encountered teachers who tried to elevate literature to a level apprehensible only by an elite few. This literature-as-a-high-mystery approach serves a couple of functions: it elevates the teacher who espouses it at the same time it excuses that teacher from having to be rigorous minded in actually thinking about the work itself. Teachers who have practiced this method have done so in large part simply because it is a centuries-old, literary-pedagogical tradition, but I tend to be personally irked about it. The message of that kind of teaching is that there is such an immense distance between literature and the student that the idea of any but the most gifted student having literary aspirations is absurd. Which is to say that I now feel that such teaching conspired to deny me and others like me our rightful literary heritage. So one of my most basic aims in the classroom is to try to return that heritage to practical minded students.

The practical approach to reading literature has direct implications for trying to write good stories and poems. Here are some of the practical aspects of writing I wish to reflect in my teaching:

Writing is a natural act. You don't have to be somebody else to write well. You do have to be yourself—or try to be yourself—to write good poems and stories. But because they've been taught that literature is so far "above them," many of my students feel that they must spout philosophical profundities, espouse noble sentiments, and compose archaically poetical phrases. In short, many of my students see the act of trying to make literature as one that by definition requires them to be other than themselves. And they aren't easily disillusionable in this regard. My project for a semester of beginning poetry- and fiction-writing may be generally described as trying to coax a room full of twenty-year-olds to try to be—or to discover—themselves in their writing.

Reading is also a natural act for a writer. Reading is writing's nourishment. Like anyone else, a writer reads for pleasure and instruction, but there is another level at which writers read: ruthlessly and automatically, they consume the writing technology of what they read. Writers learn the craft of writing by reading the work of other writers. I don't think writers of integrity steal from other writers in any direct way, but I do think they incorporate other writers' technology into their own systems. No writer of integrity would say to himself, "Ah, yes, Salinger switches from the first-person to the third-person point of view here in the middle of 'For Esme with Love and Squalor,' and I am going to write a story utilizing this very successful device." At the same time, I think that any serious writer would not read "For Esme with Love and Squalor" without remarking that change in point of view, without thinking about it, and without incorporating observations and conclusions about that device into his or her own writing technology. Imitating the device itself would be the crudest articulation of how one writer learns from another. More likely, the reading writer's point-of-view decisions will be informed by the Salinger story in only subtle ways.

Within their individual sensibilities—the true source of originality—writers carry around what they've learned from other writers. Within that part of me that is peculiar to David Huddle also reside William Faulkner, Ernest Hemingway, Peter Taylor, Eudora Welty, Flannery O'Connor, Raymond Carver, John Cheever, J. D. Salinger, Richard Yates, George P. Elliott, Hannah Green, and two or three hundred other writers. I am honored to have them as my guests.

My teaching reflects my experience of having my writing nourished by my reading, by my using anthologies in class, by my reading stories and poems aloud in class and discussing them with my writing students—in a practical kind of way. To help students with specific problems or issues in their writing, I often refer them to such and such a story, poem, book, or writer, and I lend my books to students who seem to me serious and likely to return the books.

I wish all of my discussions of writing to be informed by my reading, and I wish to demonstrate to students that I see my writing life as being carried out in the company of other writers carrying out their writing lives. I wish to demonstrate to students that I am a writer primarily because I love other writers' stories, novels, poems, and essays. Occasionally I'll put it bluntly to a student: if you don't love reading short stories, then you have no business trying to write them.

Criticism—or responding verbally to manuscripts—is a natural act. In this case, I have a two-front war to wage with my students: there are those who wish to make pronouncements about the worksheets that we discuss (e.g., "This story fails because its author stereotypes the main characters"), and there are those who feel that they are not trained critics and therefore they have no business criticizing anyone's work and furthermore an author's story is the way it is because that's how the author wanted it to be and who are they to take issue with the author's intentions?

One tactic I exercise here is that of ascribing esthetic will to literary works; I suggest that stories yearn toward a state of perfection, that it is up to an author to give a story what *it* wants or needs, and that it is up to a critic to help the author discern a story's desires. This is not nearly as much of a fairy tale as it sounds in this fast version; my own experience of writing has been one of developing sensitivity to the signals my work is giving me as I compose it. I tell my students that when I first began writing, I always had a plan and I stuck to it as strictly as possible, trying to ignore the distracting ideas that came to me in the composing process. I tell them that I still begin with a plan, but that nowadays I try to accept most of the ideas that come to me in the composing process. I tell them that such ideas are, in my opinion, true inspiration, and that I have found the inspiration that comes this way, from within the work, to be much more reliable and useful than the other kind, the kind that comes when you're taking a walk in the woods, watching a sunset, or listening to your favorite music.

A couple of other tactics I have are "pretend devices" designed to free up a critic to allow the expression of opinions that are withheld because of social inhibition. The easiest one is to ask, "Sarah, if this story were yours, what would be the first thing you'd try to change in it?" A student who would never dream of saying, "I think you ought to develop the male character," would think it perfectly all right to say, "If this were my story, I'd try to develop the male character a little more." A similar "pretend device" of mine goes this way, "Let's say this is your story, and you sent it to *The New Yorker* and they sent it back to you saying, 'We loved this story, but we think it needs to be cut by about a page and a half.' Where would you do the cutting, Sarah?" In this case, Sarah might not wish to suggest cutting the story even while pretending she wrote it, but pretending that she wrote it and that *The New Yorker* wants her to cut it will allow her to see and to say exactly where the story should be edited.

Receiving criticism may not be a natural act, but it is a valuable skill, very much worth developing. A crucial introduction to this development can be the standard workshop practice of requiring an author to be silent during the discussion of his or her work. A workshop where an author can't keep quiet but feels compelled to defend and explain the work under discussion is a counterproductive experience for both the author and the people who are trying to offer helpful criticism.

Nowadays, before a class's first workshop session, I try to set forth the ground rules in such a way as to designate the author's place in the discussion as one of privilege. I'll try to say something like, "Knowing that you will have the last say in the discussion, you authors may sit back and listen from a vantage point of serene detachment." I recommend that the author try to take notes because (1) taking notes helps you to keep your mouth shut and (2) notes help you remember useful remarks you might forget under the influence of the emotional state authors usually find themselves in when their work is discussed. I remind the class that workshop discussions are solely for the benefit of the author; they do not take place so that critics can show off for each other, and they do not take place so that an author can explain his or her work to his readers. Workshops take place so that readers can communicate to an author how his or her work has affected them and what possibilities they see within the work. I remind authors that they are not required to accept any of the criticism they are offered, and I suggest that they not be hasty in deciding whether or not to use a piece of criticism or a suggestion. A suggestion that seems insulting during and immediately after the discussion may next week be the key to a brilliant revision. Ideally, over the course of days and weeks, authors will consider the discussion of their work and will make changes at their leisure.

It is easy for a writing teacher, who might have participated in several thousand workshop sessions, to forget what a traumatic experience it can be for a student who has never, or has seldom, had the experience of having a story or poem publicly discussed. When I was a graduate student at Columbia, I was often a brutal critic of my fellow students' work; I felt personally insulted by writing I thought not to be good, I wasn't above showing off for my instructors and the other students I respected, and I figured I owed it to weak writers to discourage them from pursuing an activity that was sure to bring them disappointment. As a teacher, over the years, I have encouraged myself to try to be kinder and more positive in my criticism, especially in what I express in the public forum of the workshop. It is one thing to write a student a note about a manuscript that conveys the suggestion that a higher quality of work is in order; it is quite another to humiliate a student in a class. I try to monitor the schedule of presentations so that a student has a chance to present his or her best story to the workshop. And if something is dreadfully wrong with a story that is presented to a workshop, rather than harping on the wrongness of it, I try to persuade participants to suggest various ways of solving that problem.

In my last ten years of teaching I have learned the value of responding in writing to student manuscripts. In order to write a response to a manuscript I have to think harder about it than I would if I were speaking aloud about it in class or in a conference with the student; writing clarifies my thinking and demands that I try to make my thinking useful for the student-author. From the student's view, it helps to have a written response so that faulty memory doesn't erase or alter the instructor's observations; the tangibility of a written response can encourage a higher quality of revision. It also helps to have a written response from the instructor before a story goes before a workshop, so that a student can have some idea of how the discussion might proceed.

Out of writing responses to hundreds of manuscripts, I have developed a technique that I call "diplomatic syntax." Here's a crude example: would you rather someone said to you, "You have beautiful eyes, but you have bad breath," or "You have bad breath, but you have beautiful eyes"? The literal message of the sentence is that you have these two qualities, beautiful eyes and bad breath, but the syntax of the first example makes the bad breath more important than the beautiful eyes whereas the opposite is the case in the second example. So most of us would probably prefer to hear, "You have bad breath, but you have beautiful eyes." Getting the news that way would probably send us to brush our teeth while studying our eyes in the bathroom mirror. Getting it the other way might send us to our rooms to cry or pout.

Here's how diplomatic syntax applies to written responses to student writing. Let's say I'm trying to respond to a story that has the following qualities:

- The action is exaggerated.
- The characters are stereotypes.
- The writing is cliche-riddled.
- There is only one believable scene in the whole story.

Let's say that this is a student's first short story, and in spite of the low quality of the work, I want to be as encouraging as possible. To convey my sense of the relative importance of the story's problems, I might begin my note to the student this way:

Although you have a strong scene on page 6, you have at least three major problems to deal with here: the action is so exaggerated that a reader can't take it seriously, your characters are such stereotypes that a reader knows their lines before they say them, and you've used so many cliches that reading your prose is like eating last week's corn muffins.

As a teacher and as a writer constantly engaged in the struggle to write well, I know it's sometimes hard to resist composing that kind of note because it conveys to the student just how far away his or her work is from writing of an acceptable quality. But of course as a student, if I get a note like that about a story I've worked pretty hard on, my emotional response (of being discouraged) is likely to obliterate the illumination I might receive from that message from my teacher. So here's how a teacher might convey the same criticism but couched (an appropriate verb here) in diplomatic syntax:

Although you need to work on making the story's action more credible, developing and individualizing your characters, and freshening up your prose, you've nevertheless written a terrific scene on page 6 that demonstrates the principles you need to apply to the story's other scenes. When that girl walks out of that bar and says, "I won't be coming back to this place any more," that is an utterly believable scene, and that line of dialogue you've given her is exactly the kind of thing you need to have her saying elsewhere.

One might argue that diplomatic syntax is nothing more than sugarcoating the truth. I would counter by pointing out that a professional writer and teacher of writing has such highly developed critical faculties that encountering something wrong in a manuscript causes a mental red light to start blinking madly and a relentless inner voice to begin chanting, "Fix it! Fix it! Fix it!" But this extreme response needs to be translated into terms that are useful for a beginning writer. What the apprentice has done well quite often can be the foundation upon which to build a sense of critical values. If an apprentice can see that he or she has written one good scene, there is at least a chance that the difference between that scene and the unsuccessful scenes will become evident, and personal critical values can begin to form. Diplomatic syntax may very well be sugarcoating, but it is also a means by which the truth can be made useful for a beginning writer.

Beginning writers are not the only ones with tender feelings, though. Every semester, in my beginning poetry- and fiction-writing classes, I read one of my own stories and some of my own poems to my students. This is not a pedagogical activity for the thin-skinned. In a workshop of fifteen or sixteen people, there will always be at least one who can ask a devastating question. ("Why did that girl walk out of that bar that way?") Nowadays, I pride myself on not being defensive in class, on listening carefully to whatever is said about my work, and on making it clear that I will consider anything and everything that is said to me about my work. This is not just acting on my part; I have benefited a great deal from criticism I have received from my writing classes. But that doesn't mean that I don't often walk out of such classes with my soul bleeding. ("Didn't they understand that she walked out of the bar because of the song playing on the jukebox?")

But I'm a better writer for having submitted my writing to the workshop for scrutiny, and I hope my workshops are more nourishing communities as a result of my having brought my work into them. An important lesson I took from George Garrett, my mentor at Hollins College in 1968–69, was the value of a writer-teacher's companionship. That Garrett treated me like a writer helped me begin thinking of myself as a writer. At the time he was treating me so generously, I questioned his judgment and diminished the esteem I accorded to him. We're all familiar with that dynamic: "If he thinks I'm a writer, then he can't be all that great a writer himself." I now understand what a noble thing it is that George has done over the years for his many hundreds of writing students: he has extended himself toward us in such an absolutely democratic way as to prevent the kind of idolization that many other writing teachers encourage. By treating us as writers, he helped us become writers. Garrett's manner toward his students requires them to see him as a regular guy trying as best he can to get some good writing done, and there could certainly be no more useful example for an apprentice writer.

I've been lucky to have had a number of writing teachers whose treatment of me as a fellow artist has helped me carry out my

work. The first story-writing class I took was at the University
of Virginia in 1963 from a formidable nonwriter, Professor John
Coleman, a brittle-witted, quick-tongued guy whose practice it
was to read the students' stories aloud in class and to correct
and ridicule them as he read them. In some cases, he had the
student read his own story aloud—by coming to the front and
standing before the class—but he continued to interrupt with
corrections and comments in the course of the reading.

There were two or three of us that he favored, and I was lucky
to have received Coleman's mercy, but his general technique for
that class was to set us students against each other in seeking his
approval. U. Va. was an all-male school then, and the atmosphere
of that classroom had a kind of locker-room ruthlessness about
it. We laughed at our classmates as they were subjected to Coleman's humiliations; his teaching conspired to make us admire
him and to despise each other.

My next writing teacher was James Kraft, a young man who'd
just received his doctorate from Virginia, a very energetic and
hospitable teacher. Kraft wasn't a published writer, but he had
been working on a novel for a while, and he wasn't a cruel
teacher. I came to this class, in the summer of 1967, straight out
of the army's 25th Military Intelligence Detachment stationed
in Cu Chi, Vietnam, and of course what I was writing then were
stories about my military experience. Between being discharged
from the army in Oakland, California, and coming to Char-
lottesville, I'd spent a week with my parents in Louisville, Ken-
tucky, sunbathing by their apartment complex swimming pool
and trying to impress the lifeguard, a pretty high school girl
named Nancy. In my heroic efforts, I'd dived into water that
was too shallow and had skinned my nose rather dramatically.
As a result of my week of civilian life, I showed up in Jim Kraft's
class as this Vietnam Vet looking dark-skinned and recently
wounded, as if I'd just stepped out of the jungle with a string
of Vietcong ears attached to my belt. Kraft and the other students
treated me with a rather horrified respect, and whatever I might
have written, they were not likely to criticize it harshly. I wasn't
writing stories with much authenticity, but Kraft addressed my
work with a seriousness that always surprised me. I remember
that the one nonmilitary story I wrote had a character in it named
Leviticus—simply because I liked the sound of that name. Preparing for class the night before that story came up for discussion, Kraft read the entire book of Leviticus, trying to

understand my Biblical allusion. If he was irked when I told him that I had no reason other than the sound of it for using that name, he didn't let on. From him I learned as a writer not to be careless in my choices and as a would-be teacher that taking a student's writing seriously encourages the student to take it seriously, too.

Peter Taylor was my next writing teacher, for his first and my last two semesters at the University of Virginia. Though I later came to revere him, in 1967 Taylor was no one I'd ever heard of before. He had a kind of humble, shambling air about him that did not encourage veneration. In class his manner was without authority. He brought in books and read aloud from them, mostly Chekhov, though I also heard him read Faulkner's "That Evening Sun" and Caroline Gordon's "Old Red" and a fair portion of Katherine Ann Porter's "Old Mortality." He spoke about characters and scenes the way you'd talk about things that happened in your family or among your friends. This was in a graduate-level class—he had been kind enough to let me enroll in it—and for about the first month and a half, he read to us in class and talked with us in this unsettlingly ordinary way about what he'd read. I had handed in a couple of stories, and I was impatient to have them discussed in class, and I knew that several other students were even more disturbed than I was at Taylor's unproductive use of our class time.

Taylor held conferences with some of us about stories. He had an office in a little, dimly lit, musty smelling house on the other side of Jefferson Park Avenue from Cabell Hall, and over there, too, he seemed to me to lack the exotic aura I expected a real writer to have. It was sort of like going into your uncle's law office and talking about your plans for perhaps attending law school. Taylor did not go over your manuscript sentence by sentence. Rather, he spoke generally about disappointingly non-literary issues of the story and about fiction writing in general. A couple of things I remember his telling me were that it was awfully hard finding what you wanted to write about and that he had been grateful to see that his subject matter was family. He also told me once of his father's being mad at him about a story he wrote that had a character in it very much like a family aunt; his father had met him at the airport shortly after the story's publication and told him that if Taylor had been around when the father read it, the father would have hit him. He told me that he sometimes left blanks in his stories when he couldn't think of the right word or the right sentence; he said that he liked going over and over his stories because it gave them a kind of "gnarled" quality.

Mr. Taylor requested a conference with me to talk about one of my stories that I'd been especially eager to have discussed in class. Its denouement came in a scene where a man and a woman are engaged in sex in the female-superior position on a kitchen table when the woman's husband comes in and murders her with a shotgun. Now that I remember it, it seems to me that Mr. Taylor took me into a small room behind his office for our conference, and it became evident to me that talking about this story embarrassed him a great deal, but he gave me to understand it was a lesser embarrassment than trying to lead a discussion of it in class would have been. One of the things he said then was that he personally had nothing against a dirty story— he claimed to have written a few of them himself—but that he didn't think a person who might not wish to read such a story ought to have one inflicted on him- or herself in a workshop. If that session sticks in my mind, it also sticks in Peter's. From then on, over the years, whenever anyone reported back to me that they'd seen Peter Taylor and mentioned my name to him, they'd say he shook his head over the kind of stories I was writing in those days. So far as I know, Peter still thinks of me as a quasi-pornographer.

When Peter finally did get around to discussing our stories in class, he took it upon himself to read them aloud to us. He said that he thought it would be useful for us to hear our stories read in another voice and to hear all of them read in the same voice. Well, he was right about that, you could hear things about your story when he read it that wouldn't have been evident otherwise. If he had trouble with a sentence, you knew it needed some reworking; if he read a passage as if he savored it, you knew you'd done something right. Again, his actual talk about our stories was so ordinary and commonsensical that it frustrated me and frustrated most of us. We'd jump in with negative observations whenever possible, and Peter let us have our say, but most often he was in the position of defending a story against the criticism of the majority of the class. At the time, this way of running a class seemed to me all wrong and further evidence that Peter Taylor wasn't much of a writer and wasn't really suited to be a writing teacher.

In spite of his reservations over my subject matter, most unobtrusively Peter Taylor brought about a personal relationship with me that I think in some part was calculated to enable me to know him, to know something about his life as a writer.

Peter also engaged my services to stay at their home while he and his wife were out of town and to look after their son, Ross, an eighth-grader. Each evening I was to take Ross to the university cafeteria for dinner and each morning to drive him to school. The Taylors' was a large house, with almost every room full of books, a house in which I passed many hours just picking up this book and that, reading bits and pieces, reading and thinking about the many inscriptions I encountered in them. Peter's study was one of the smallest rooms in the house, fairly tidy, with an old manual typewriter and a ladder-back chair. Yes, I did sit down in the chair; no, I did not try out the typewriter. Remember, I really didn't have a great deal of regard for Peter's work back then. I'd read a couple of stories, and they seemed awfully dry to me—nothing very interesting ever transpired on the kitchen table. But passing hours in that house of immense quiet and solitude, I came to feel a regard for the writing lives he and Eleanor carried out there. When the Taylors got back home, Peter had a kind of abashed exuberance about him, as if he were embarrassed at having been away to enjoy himself.

My regard for Peter Taylor's work and his teaching has increased over the years, and I now see that even at the time I was in his classes, I was learning more than I thought I was. For one thing, it was the first genuine workshop I'd attended, the difference being that we students were encouraged to form bonds with each other, even if some of the bonding came out of our impatience with Peter. John Coleman and Jim Kraft had been good writing teachers for me, but their's had been writing *classes*—in that the channels of energy went from student to professor and back from professor to student—not *workshops*—in which the class is a community of writers working with each other under the leadership of a senior writer.

After Peter Taylor at U. Va. and George Garrett at Hollins, I entered Columbia University's MFA Program where my first teacher was Richard Elman, a quintessential New York City Writer. I'd done a good deal of writing the summer before I moved to New York, and so I brought in about 125 pages of new work to show my new writing teacher. A few days later, Elman held a conference with me in which he told me very bluntly that if I was going to write like that, he would have no interest in me throughout my time at Columbia. This was pretty devastating for me, because at considerable sacrifice and expense, my wife and I had moved to the city so that I could attend Columbia, and now Columbia, in the voice of Richard Elman, was telling me before I even got started that I was a failure. My opinion is that that was a pretty reckless thing for a teacher to do to a student. Elman's point, as I now understand it, was that I was trying to rely more on craft than on heart, and somewhere along the line I did need to have that news delivered to me. I spent a month or so feeling pretty lousy about it, but then I started writing my way out of my doldrums. I felt like I had survived an assault on my writing life, and I felt stronger for having done so. So even though I would probably not be so blunt as Elman was to me, I give him credit for having done something for me that a writing teacher can sometimes do for a student, get him back on the right track.

Hannah Green was my second writing teacher at Columbia. Compared with Richard Elman, Hannah was an angel of positive reinforcement and kept a very low-profile presence in the workshop. Among her rare qualities was her capacity to be affected by what she heard or read in class. She responded very emotionally to workshop work, and she was unembarrassed about her responses, valuable behavior for me to witness, since I had schooled myself in the Faulkner-Hemingway ethic of holding back emotion as both a personal and a literary code. One particular memory of Hannah that I hold very close is of sitting beside her during Tillie Olsen's visit to our class and Tillie's reading of "Hey Sailor, What Ship?" The story is about the pain of an alcoholic's destruction witnessed by people who have loved and respected him, and while I sat listening to it, I found my eyes focused on Hannah's wrist, which at some time in her life had been broken and had healed at a slightly crooked angle. I was also aware of some small sounds Hannah made as we listened to the story together, quiet Oh's and Um's that registered the story's hurt. I of course didn't weep because of the story, but Hannah did, openly and unashamedly. In some part I feel that Hannah Green legitimized my emotional involvement in my reading and in my teaching, and she reinforced the value I'd already taken from Taylor and Garrett, that a writer's company was at least as valuable as his or her classroom teaching.

The one truly bad writing teacher I have ever had was Anthony Burgess, who was working for both Columbia and Princeton in the same term and was living in New Jersey. His reputation was that he would take no student manuscript home to read and would hold no office hours with any student. A few aggressive ones gave him rides to and from the airport in order to have some personal contact with him. He was always late for his classes, and he seemed to blame us for it; once he came in almost an hour late and shouted at us, who had sat around the seminar table waiting for him, "I don't know what you people want from me!" He left early whenever he could get by with it. During class time he went around the seminar table, holding mini-conferences with students, looking at a page of their work, skimming down that page until he found a word choice that he wished to discuss with that student. He would hold forth for a while on a particular word, and then he would go on to the next student. After three weeks of Burgess, I managed to transfer out of his class and back to Richard Elman's; Elman might have been a reckless teacher, but at least he didn't try to rip us off. Nevertheless, I learned about teaching from Burgess the way you can learn about writing by reading a really lousy book.

Lore Segal was my writing teacher for my final semester at Columbia. This was during a time when Lore was recovering from the loss of her husband David to a heart attack. She wasn't sleeping very well that spring, and she spent her hours of insomnia annotating the thesis manuscripts of those of her students who were graduating. Lore made it clear that she liked my stories, but my god did she give them a going-over with her editing pencil. From her, I learned a view of teaching writing that connects liking somebody's work with giving it the most painstaking scrutiny. For me, this continues to be a necessary principle since my natural lazy inclination is to think that if I like something, it probably doesn't need much editorial attention from me. I'm still a pretty lousy manuscript annotator, but I do have Lore's good example firmly planted in my brain.

This has been a roundabout way of demonstrating that my own teachers' primary gifts to me were not the exotic secrets of writing but were in fact the ordinary methods of living a writing life and making human connections with other writers. One of the things I have had most trouble in grasping is the letting-go part of the connections between writer-friends. For years I wrote letters to Peter Taylor dutifully reporting to him my professional progress. Once or twice I got a politely phrased postcard from him, but never a letter. On the teacher side of things, I'm still corresponding with so many of my old students that letter writing often gets in the way of my own writing. So there is a letting-go component that goes with being writer-friends with somebody that I have yet to get the hang of.

A writing workshop is, in its ideal sense, a community of writers trying to help each other accomplish their best writing. Its first level of value is in its being a community, a gathering of people whose company nourishes each person's writing life. What a workshop is not is a committee that repairs faulty manuscripts. Most of the time manuscripts can be improved through sensitive revision in response to workshop discussion. But the process is not a mechanical one in which critics tell the author what is wrong with a story and how to fix it, and the author goes home and does what the workshop told him to do. The dynamic of a workshop is oblique, indirect, subtle, and occasionally perverse. Listening to workshop discussion of one story may lead an author to a realization of how to write another, much more urgently felt story. Listening to workshop discussion of a story's ending may bring the author to a solution of a problem with the story's beginning, of which only the author is aware. I believe that workshops can be immensely useful but that they are only rarely useful in obvious and logical ways. I also believe that their usefulness is strongly determined by their members' level of community commitment. Writers caring enough about the work of other writers to give it their time and attention has a generally nourishing effect on the work of both.

Some of the most valuable things I have been taught as a writer are intangibles that have come out of my having carried on my work in the company of other writers carrying on their work. These are values that I hope to pass on to my students, both in and out of workshops, through example, through mental telepathy, through having these values inform everything that I say about writing. These are elements of a writers' code, and though I can't articulate them all, I can nevertheless give you an idea of what I'm talking about:

- The one relationship that counts is that between you and your writing. If you feel good about what you're working on, then you're in good shape, and if you don't feel good about it, then you need to figure out what to change so that you do feel good about it. What you're working on right now is what matters, not what you have written and not what you're going to write.

- Writing is writing's reward. The best part of story-writing is to be working on a story in which you are wholeheartedly and wholemindedly engaged. The support and encouragement of friends, family, and/or even strangers can help, but finally you have to find your reasons for doing it *in doing it.*
- Write for the good of the work—as opposed to writing for others or writing for self.
- Serve your stories relentlessly by doing everything you can to make them as good as you can make them (e.g., letting others read them, trying to revise them to perfection, carrying out appropriate research instead of trying to fake it).
- Write stories you *want* to live with. This isn't always possible— or it's hard to know if a story you're working on will become one you want to live with. You have to write a number of stories that you need to cast off from yourself and not live with. But it's useful to remind yourself that your reason for writing these things is because you want certain stories of your own to live in the world with you.
- Write often enough that you miss it if you don't do it. To have a real writing life, you must be writing at least this often. Going to your writing should seem a pleasure rather than a burden to you; if it isn't a pleasure, then you need to shape up your writing life.
- Demand of yourself that you grow in your ability, your ambition, your achievement. If you don't feel you're getting somewhere in your writing, then you need to make some changes. Grow or rot, those are your choices. It is one of the happy functions of the writing workshop—the community of your writer-friends—to keep you growing.

III

DILEMMAS

*. . . ongoing conflicts about
creativity, competence vs.
excellence, guiding
dissertations, authenticity
of voice, limited time,
and writer's block*

13

The Poet as Teacher: Vices and Virtues

STEPHEN DUNN

Stephen Dunn is the author of seven collections of poetry, including **Between Angels** *(Norton, 1989) and* **Local Time** *(Morrow), winner of the National Poetry Series Open Competition in 1986. His awards include a Guggenheim Fellowship, three NEA Creative Writing Fellowships, the Levinson Prize from* **Poetry,** *and the Theodore Roethke Prize from* **Poetry Northwest.** *His work has appeared in* **The New Yorker, The Nation, The Atlantic, Antaeus,** *and* **The American Poetry Review,** *to name a few. He is Professor of Creative Writing at Stockton State College in New Jersey.*

An obvious given: In this country a poet must have another job. A few poets, very few, can eke out a living from doing readings, but certainly no poet's royalties are sufficient to live on. I've long ago accepted this as the way things are. I teach. I get paid for talking about what I like to talk about, and I wish it were that simple. When I was asked by a colleague to write something about how, if at all, the teaching of poetry writing has affected my own writing, my first thought was, "Maybe it has a little, but not importantly." It was my second thought too, but increasingly the question seemed to deserve a more elaborate answer.

One of the things I hear myself saying over and again to my

poetry-writing students is "Your poem effectively begins at the first moment you've surprised or startled yourself. Throw away everything that preceded that moment, and begin with that moment." I go on to say that we mostly begin our poems with our ordinary, workaday minds, those minds burdened by the conventional, and if we're lucky we start to say something we didn't know we knew, and/or find phrasing that couldn't have been available to us at the outset of the poem. If we do, then we're on our way. Having said that, it's chastening to note that Frost said that anyone can get into a poem, it takes a poet to get out of one.

To the extent that the ability to isolate problem areas in other people's poems draws the teaching poet's attention to the same problems in his or her own poems, I suppose that the teaching of poetry writing for all these years has contributed in some way to my own work. But the question of whether the teaching of writing affects one's own work raises other issues; among them, competence versus excellence, and the nature of poetry itself. Personally, I can't see how it hurts, unless the regular encounter with bad poetry can be argued to be harmful, or, as I'll elaborate on later, one's teaching starts to take precedence over one's writing. On the other hand, if we wish to write truly memorable poems, which I do and most poets do, then I can't see how the teaching of poetry writing helps very much. George Seferis wrote, "To say what you want to say, you must create another language and nourish it for years with what you have loved, with what you have lost, with what you will never find again." In light of such a remark, teaching poetry seems separate indeed from the real stuff that goes into the making of a poem.

I suspect that if I aspired to be a competent poet, then the teaching of writing would help me to be just that. That is, a master of various kinds of decorum, a manager of certain pleasures, alert to the ungenuine, the downright false. But competence, the ability to fashion what looks like a poem and even to please, is the bugaboo of the creative writing teacher qua poet, and the enterprise of creative writing itself. The danger is that we can become satisfied with making things turn out satisfactorily. The well-made poem, lacking the Seferis ingredients, is increasingly in my own work what I try to avoid, though I'm sure I fail more than succeed.

In my poetry-writing workshops on the undergraduate level, I'm happy at first with competence. On the graduate level I try not to be. Over the years it's been important for me to think about why I'm in this profession at all. After all, so few of my students have turned out to be poets. If I'm not making writers, what am I doing?

First, some assumptions about language and the importance of precision. Most of the language we encounter daily is imprecise if not consciously designed to deceive. We constantly are confronted with versions of the world that don't correspond to our sense of it. On one of its levels, a poetry workshop infuses and restores a respect for precision, for finding the right words, therefore moving the writer closer to what can credibly be said about something. This is one reason why teaching still pleases me; over, say, a semester, to witness a student move in the direction of the true(r). I treat even the most marginal student's poem as a poem wishing to be a poem. I hold it to high standards, as if it might be a poem. But secretly what I know I'm doing is instructing the student about the tendency toward self-indulgence (the main problem of beginning writers), the problems of sloppy feeling and thinking, and something about what the inauthentic sounds like. It's moral instruction in the guise of crafting and editing. When teaching graduate students, all of whom are there because they wish to be poets, I'm doing the same thing, though I'm less tolerant of the merely competent poem, and seek and hold out for those distinguishing characteristics that might separate them from the horde. But in fact the major thrust of my teaching has to do with accuracy and truthfulness, which implies surprising oneself and having enough savvy to know what might surprise others. Even when a student fails to write a startling poem, there are often moments in the poem to praise—movements toward the genuine. If I remember that this is mostly what I'm doing as a teacher, helping them to move toward and identify the genuine, then I'm less disappointed when the marginal students, quite properly, decide to become social workers instead. And of course, too, the entire process makes all of them better readers. Most of my academic colleagues will attest that the creative writing students are among their most alert readers, sensitive to the ways poems and stories move and turn.

As everyone knows, you can't teach someone to be a poet. At best, you offer cautionary advice as it applies to specific, practical problems, perhaps citing a great poet's successful handling of the same problem. You praise the student's true achievements.

You assign and discuss great and good poems and urge students to find their own models of excellence. Maybe you tell them some of the compelling statements writers have made about being writers, which go beyond just wanting to be wordsmiths. Gunter Kunert's: "That's why I write; to bear the world as it crumbles..." Or Rilke's: "The ultimate intuitions and insights will only approach one who lives in his work and remains there, and whoever considers them from afar gains no power over them." Yet when I try to recall what I've said in workshops, I mostly remember not the highminded things I've said but the many *be carefuls* that I've offered. Be careful of the first line that's longer or shorter than the line you've been working with; it may signal that you've fallen out of rhythm. Be careful of the first moment that you double back and return to a previous effect; it may mean that you've ceased to advance the poem, or have nothing more to say. Be careful of an ending that seems only satisfactory; there's a better one sleeping in your material if you hold out for it. Be careful that this poem truly matters to you; otherwise think of it as practice and put it aside. Be careful not to be too careful in first drafts; let the poem go, let it always find its next moment, hope that it gets away from you. These are things I've said to students for years, and now and then I listen to my own precepts. A good teacher can hasten a potential poet's development, not much more. As far as his own work goes, good teaching might help to make him a better reviser, a better editor, not much more.

A well-known poet once said that when he taught a very good class it often set his writing back a week or so. He was referring to the tremendous satisfaction that comes from teaching well. Writers, I think, know this better than nonwriters because there's a common principle involved. When you teach well you start to say things you didn't know you were going to say, perhaps things you had forgotten you knew. That kind of discovery is exactly what happens in a good poem or story. After teaching well, the poet feels less urgency to go home and write. We need enormous energy both to teach and write well.

Sometimes the poet-teacher is simply beleaguered, involved in poorly paid part-time work, and/or compelled to move from job to job, state to state, almost every year. And most junior professors find themselves with many papers to grade, classes to prepare, committees to endure. In such cases, "teaching" is not the issue. It's all the demands of getting ready to teach, plus tertiary collegial obligations. There's a debilitating encroachment on writing time.

Even in good situations, the human factors in teaching poetry writing take considerable emotional energy. It's the most intimate teaching I've ever done. Though I try to treat all poems as if they were fictions, I know I'm talking about someone's life, and/or someone's creation in which there's a large ego investment. Even the most delicate criticisms hurt. At the same time, I'm aware that few other people, give or take a few shrinks, will ever again take these would-be poets' personal revelations so seriously. There's a large responsibility in that. I want them to find their hidden subject. I want them to say things they didn't know they knew, and I want them to say those things precisely and surprisingly. Students are startled when they reveal their most haunting secrets and, instead of making judgments about them, you say perhaps, "Stained would be a better word than bloody in this line." Or perhaps, more cruelly, "You've yet to make the abortion interesting for others. You haven't yet gotten beyond the confessional impulse." It's a violation of intimacy (and poor pedagogy) to discuss the personal revelation as revelation. The best intimacy between teacher and student occurs when the student trusts that the teacher is some kind of partner in helping the poem in question to become a poem. But more often, even if there is trust, the student clings to his or her creation, is not ready to hear the things that are wrong with it. It even can be argued that the students *should* cling to their creations for as long as they can; after all, some kind of gumption is going to be needed to get through the coming years of neglect. Yet for the teacher to address such understandable if unearned pride, face to face in workshops and in conferences, can be exhausting and harrowing work.

Even though I teach in a state college and do not have a cushy teaching load, I've been lucky to have a teaching schedule that affords me my mornings free. I can't complain. Teaching, on the face of it, has been better for me than most jobs would have been. I don't subscribe to the manual labor theory, popular during the sixties. To wit, work a job in which you don't use your brain, as if that would grant you greater purity and brain-power when you sat down to write. Mostly, manual labor makes you tired and therefore represents a different encroachment on time, and purity is something few of us ever achieve. In fact, purity for the writer may not be very desirable. Complicity always has seemed more seminal to me.

Much has been written of late about university life being injurious to the spirit and about the way it might limit the kinds of experience one might bring to a poem. There's some truth in such claims. But most of life is injurious to the spirit, and the "real world" is often as limiting as the university. The writer's burden is somehow to keep alive and vital amid all that's dangerous and deadening in the world, and this is difficult wherever one is. Stevens managed it in an insurance firm. Eliot (for a while) in a bank. The imagination is a friend of the spirit, and it travels awfully well; it really doesn't mind when you take it to a dull party. That may be exactly where it comes into its own.

In Roethke's wonderful poem "Dolor," for example, we see the verve and the cohering powers of the poet's imagination as it takes on institutional life.

Dolor

I have known the inexorable sadness of pencils,
Neat in their boxes, dolor of pad and paperweight,
All the misery of manilla folders and mucilage,
Desolation in immaculate public places,
Lonely reception room, lavatory, switchboard,
The unalterable pathos of basin and pitcher,
Ritual of multigraph, paper-clip, comma,
Endless duplication of lives and objects.
And I have seen the dust from the walls of institutions
Finer than flour, alive, more dangerous than silica,
Sift, almost invisible, through long afternoons
                    of tedium,
Dropping a fine film on nails and delicate eyebrows,
Glazing the pale hair, the duplicate gray standard
                    faces.

Not to become one of "the duplicate gray standard faces" takes vigilance; it's a teacher's problem as much as it is an account executive's or a clerk's. And it's a writer's problem as well, not to become one of the gray, standard writers. To finally write like no one else. So few of us achieve such singularity that it would be foolish to blame the university for our failure to do so. This is why I find it difficult to say exactly what, if anything, teaching has meant to my writing. The clearest thing it's done is give me more time than if I'd had another job.

The rest is between the poet and the gods. It may come down to something as undemocratic and undiscussable as talent. Who knows? The good poet always surmounts circumstances, both the circumstances of his or her life and the initial circumstances of his or her poem. This is why mere competence is the enemy of good poetry. Every good poem is evidence of a step taken into the unknown or the vaguely known, from which one comes back with palpable approximations. Words for. Much apprenticeship and practice are needed to get to the point where such a step can be taken (Keats and Rimbaud notwithstanding). The act of getting there can't be taught, nor can it be willed.

Teaching is one kind of mastery, one way of knowing and becoming intimate with your subject. As I said earlier, I don't think it can hurt your writing as long as you remain more of a poet than a teacher. That's the difficult balance. When the scale tips toward teaching as your primary identity, when the struggles and pleasures of the classroom supercede the struggles and pleasures of the page, as can easily happen, that's when you must rightly call yourself teacher, an honorable enough title to be sure, but a capitulation to safer territory in which a text already exists and there's no permanent record of what you've said.

It's no accident that more good poetry arises out of crises and dilemmas than out of triumphs and jobs well done. We are less likely to confront self and world when we're satisfied with self and world. We're less likely to have that edge that leads to discovery. The poet always must be to some degree an outsider, must always be probing for what's hidden and unexplored, must always resist what passes for reality. Most poets I know don't have to be willful about this. It's a matter of temperament. Kafka's Hunger Artist, when asked why he became the way he was, said he just didn't like that food the rest of us eat. Kafka's parable suggests that the artist must be driven by obsessions and needs that are not necessarily located in the rational domain. They constitute the artist's strength against the manifold pulls toward the conventional and the great middle. This may be why few poets are granted tenure. On the other hand, the university poet who buys in too fully to being a good citizen of the university is in danger of losing his outsider's edge.

In my case, since I'm mostly inclined to be a good citizen, I'm occasionally saved by other limitations of my personality. It's not that I don't like the university's food, it's just that I don't possess the ability to eat it very well. For example, when I've found myself on committees, I rarely know what to say. Once, finding myself on something called "The Priorities & Resources Committee," I vainly tried to think in those terms. My colleagues construed my silence as arrogance, but in fact it was incompetence. This kind of thing has happened often enough that I'm seldom asked to be on committees. When I am, I marvel at those who find the proper words for the occasion. Other times, my inclinations to be solitary, to withdraw, are immense. I suspect, for better or worse, these are perceived as the quirks of the poet.

Because I teach *creative writing*, it's important for me to remember that I'm not a *creative writer*, I'm a poet. It's important for me to remember to tell my students that I'm not interested in *creative* writing; I'm interested in poetry. There are many creative writers, and relatively few poets. I receive many interesting inventions. I receive many well-made verbal machines. Rarely do I receive that "clear expression of mixed feelings," that blend of "delight and wisdom," that piece of writing that "takes the top of my head off," which is poetry. Rather than find this too dispiriting, often I can take pleasure in small improvements and the flashes of the genuine that students are capable of. Granted, some days it doesn't seem worth it. At those times I need to remember that, in the relative scheme of things, a small community of would-be poets is a rather tolerable place to hang out.

In the final analysis, how a fine poem comes along is mysterious, though when it happens it's clearly a transcendence of what one's job may be, even if that "job" is lucky enough to be poet and nothing else. How many times does lightning strike? How many times does the poet get to traffic with the gods? Away from lightning, light years away from the gods, the teaching of poetry isn't a bad occupation. It may be argued that lightning hits the person in the field more than it hits the person in the university. Maybe. But the poet who teaches lives in the field too, inescapably, in the common field of love and loss and sorrow, not to mention revenge, ambiguity, deception, etc. And the gods, I have to believe, are perverse and ubiquitous, though no doubt more likely to visit those of us who habitually try to reach them.

14

Solitude and Confusion and Awe

JOYCE GREENBERG LOTT

Joyce Greenberg Lott teaches English at South Brunswick High School in New Jersey. She is one of the organizers of **Project Promise,** *an alternative school for potential high school dropouts, and is currently designing and team teaching an interdisciplinary humanities elective for seniors. Her poems have appeared in* **Stone Country, US1, Eleven,** *and* **Journal of New Jersey Poets,** *and her article on "Not Teaching Poetry" appeared in* **English Journal** *(April, 1989).*

I am a full-time teacher and a sometimes poet. For years, something in my life seemed to be blocking the poems. It has taken me a long time to realize that it wasn't an obstacle so much as an absence, not what stopped me but what wasn't there to get me started. The best label I can put on what was missing is "solitude and confusion and awe." Once I came to understand the importance of these factors in my own writing life, I was much clearer about trying to create them in the classroom.

The first poem I wrote after five years of not writing poetry came as I was flying home from visiting my parents in Florida. The previous year I had seen my father in a hospital bed, and now he had made a miraculous recovery. My thoughts were a jumble: my parents' age, our distance from each other, my own sense of homelessness in their new condo. I wasn't sure what I was feeling. All I knew was that I needed to write.

But even traveling alone, I found it hard to take out the notepad I had snitched from my mother's kitchen counter. The pad meant ignoring the people sitting on either side of me, stifling the friendliness my parents had taught me. But I did.

Revisiting My Parents

Having passed their seventy-sixth birthdays
My parents are more considerate
to each other, kinder. Coordinated
leisure wear covers the bruises they got
as they pushed each other to reach this place,
their vision of the top.

Seventy-six years and more than a thousand miles
separate the dark stairways and overstuffed sofas
of my parents' birthplaces
from the chrome and glass of their present existence.

No hairs from Zeda's beard lie damp and disorderly
in the corners of my mother's shower;
only once did I hear echoes of Bubble's accent
in the exercise room of my father's clubhouse.

I might eulogize that our family history has died
in this rebuilt swamp, but I know better.
History continues: one place leads to another—
Austria to New York to New Jersey to Florida.
Our family landscape changes
like the ancient story of the wandering Jew.

Yet somehow landscape is simpler to name
than people. The symmetry of my parents' balcony
overlooking Florida flatness.
Egrets feeding at the man-made lagoon below.

Last week I visited people I have known for fifty years—
my parents—in a place unconnected to me,
except for them, and they've changed:
for the better, for the kinder, for the easier.

No matter what has been lost or left behind
over all those years and miles—

isn't that some sort of miracle
after all?

I was elated; never mind how "good" it was, I finally started a poem again. But the only place I had been able to write was in the sky, suspended, and even there it had been hard to give myself permission.

For my whole adult life I have had trouble allowing myself to write. I can only guess why: my compulsiveness at work, my need to be outside and active, my family's belief that making money is what matters. But even as I go through my guesses, I sound like a negative student blaming everyone from his cousin to his dog, except that for me, it's my job, my family, myself.

I wasn't always like this. I remember the first time I really wrote as vividly as I remember my first real kiss. I was in the sixth grade and had pinkeye. The school nurse declared me contagious and sent me home. During that week of officially sanctioned solitude I rode my bike all over Absecon Island, from my house in Ventnor, New Jersey. I rode from the Inlet to Longport, stopping at the jetties and pausing to contemplate the ocean or the bay at all the beautiful spots I discovered along the way. By the third day or so, somehow I got the idea to take a pencil and a pad with me—my first poem, paraphrased, seen through pink eyes: "The sun casts her most sparkling diamonds for the ocean's wardrobe."

Forty years later, I can still see that tall, awkward ten-year-old pick her way over the rocks as she smelled the stagnant sea pools in the crevices, and, never having heard of Byron, stand up straight for probably the first time in her life, at the tip of a jetty, with her dumb contagious disease, and know in her bones that she wanted to write. Sheepishly, I realize that now, living on less than an acre of land that is being built up all around me, I am still that same romantic who needs a sense of solitude to begin to write.

This is not to say that I cannot work at my writing under other conditions. In fact, the opposite is true. Once I start writing, I expand and delete and worry over the least word, even when I'm "supposed" to be doing something else. But the unstructured time, the silence to hear myself, the imposed stillness that allows me to *begin* to write—this is what has so often been missing in my life.

My first foray as a writer was followed by prize-winning high school essays: "The Best Way to Achieve Dental Health," "What the Constitution Means to Me," and finally, my awe-inspiring graduation speech about Atlantic City High School graduates sailing out on the sea of life. I remember playing with metaphors even though I didn't know what they were called; I remember the black scrapbook my father kept of the clippings from the *Atlantic City Press* each time I won a $25 savings bond; I remember enjoying writing alone in my room with the door shut more than I enjoyed anything we studied in school.

After graduating, I went off to Wellesley College where the poet Philip Booth was my freshman English teacher. He selected a story of mine for the literary magazine but he didn't choose me as the freshman editor because he said he didn't know if I was a writer or not: I might be, but he wasn't sure. I'd like to tell you that I gobbled up knowledge, polished my writing during the wee hours of the morning, and graduated from Wellesley to prove Philip Booth wrong. But instead, I married my home-town boyfriend in June of my freshman year, was told by the dean that I could not continue to attend Wellesley as a married woman (it was the fifties, don't forget!), and almost totally ignored what had previously given me pleasure. Instead of creating literary masterpieces, I created beautifully imperfect children and had little time for anything else.

But sometimes when my son was napping and my two daughters were invited to play at a friend's house, I watched birds poised on telephone wires in front of my window and scribbled lines lamenting the fact that I would never get to go anywhere.

Where I went, after I got beyond diapers and carpooling, was back to school and eventually into teaching. I wrote some but never consistently. Instead, I crowded my life with a progression of people and activities that took up the space I would have needed to begin each new poem.

As a high school English teacher I have more than a hundred students in five periods, five days a week. Among them are two potential suicides, several drug users, fifteen who have been made crazy by grade-hungry parents, and at least fifty who let me know daily that they would rather be anyplace else but in school. I arrive home tired, frustrated, irritable, concerned about individual students, needing to prepare five classes, and always carrying at least one set of papers to grade. Rarely within this schedule is there a moment to experience the almost airborne awe that dictates my writing.

It is precisely this dilemma that I bring with me into the classroom, and I now work hard to give my students what I am only sporadically able to give myself—the solitude, confusion, and awe that may help them experience the internal urge to write and the satisfaction that writing can offer.

Because of my own lack of time and space, I am sharply aware of the displacement my students must feel as they move by the bell from class to class. Truly, no space is theirs. Although I can hardly provide Virginia Woolf's "room of one's own" for my hundred and some students, I do offer a little chunk of undisturbed writing time almost every day. My students bring their journals to class with them and, during most forty-five-minute periods, we do approximately ten minutes of journal writing about something we have been reading or discussing in class. I write in my journal when they write in theirs. It isn't exactly solitude, but it offers a safe few moments to let in the confusion and see where it leads.

Recently in a senior film elective, my student Amy discovered the power of succumbing to confusion and letting herself be overwhelmed by an experience. As I was showing Cimino's film "The Deer Hunter," she was upset by the violence and asked if she had to keep watching. I didn't say she had to, but I did tell her that the Vietnam War was real and that it might be a good experience for her to watch the movie and then write about it. After attempting several essays and realizing that her thoughts were fragmentary and conflicting, Amy wrote the following poem:

Tell Me Again

"A good experience," they say.
Maybe so, but I cannot fathom
That rude awakening.
Help me to understand the lust for power
That seizes and changes the body
Into an alien form of merciless evil.
War is no better than Hell;
A deer hunter is, no less, a man hunter.

I am naive and unworldly and ignorant,
But not stupid.
I have witnessed the blemish in human nature
But did not know its strength
Until now . . .

I writhe and twist and scream within.
Still my eyes are focused ("A good experience").
I dream and fantasize as the grass is green.
I watch the greyness and crimson,
And I question the validity of dreams.
The dreamer is a corpse;
War, its resurrection.

                    Amy Harris (4/6/89)

Amy had written very few poems before this; in fact, she told me that the reason she had been trying to write an essay was that she never knew that poems could be personal. She was pleased with the result, had worked much harder on it (four hours of revision!) than on any essay. Like her teacher on the airplane, Amy had discovered the power of language to give form and shape to confusion.

I try to invoke this power in class discussion as well as in writing, sometimes a tricky balance in high school where teachers are hired to be authority figures and to keep control. I promote confusion by waiting a long time after I ask a question and by encouraging my students to search for their own answers. And, as foolhardy as it may seem, I enjoy risky topics. When one of my sophomores, Lisa, said in discussion that Gene, the narrator of *A Separate Peace*, was gay, I encouraged the controversy that erupted and asked Lisa to find evidence to support her interpretation, as outrageous as I thought it was. Similarly, when we read Alice Walker's *The Color Purple*, I challenged my students' image of God and asked them to clarify beliefs that some of them had never examined. Paul Sackaroff, one of my former students, describes the effects of this technique in his answer to a final exam question. The question I asked was "If learning is changing, what have you learned?" Here's part of Paul's answer:

An important measure of a superior work of literature is its ability to produce in the reader a sort of healthy state of confusion and disquietude. My exposure to new types of readings, class discussion, and journal writing succeeded in creating this state of mind in me. I learned that confusion is the key to education. My state of confusion provoked me to search for firmer footing to secure myself. Thinking put me in a perspective of uncertainty and ambivalency. That's when I started to doubt preconceived answers and began to grow.

Paul mentions the same conditions that allow me to write. Last winter's visit to my parents produced this same "healthy state of confusion and disquietude" in me and as Paul said, "provoke[d] me to search for firmer footing to secure myself." For me, this footing became a poem, a series of words lined up in stanzas that gave form to my "uncertainty and ambivalency."

For Paul and Amy, who knows? Maybe someday they will make the bestseller list, or do academic articles or reports with relish, or keep an ongoing journal—or just get on a plane one day and write something that gives form to their confusion, and feel good. As a teacher and writer, I can live with that.

15

Scribblings on Writing in Economics

STEPHEN M. GOLDFELD

Stephen M. Goldfeld is a Professor of Economics at Princeton University. He is the author or co-author of six books and some seventy-five articles. Largely as a result of stints as a department chairman and as a Member of the Council of Economic Advisers, he has also written countless memos, an art form that he feels deserves more recognition. He currently holds a Guggenheim fellowship to pursue research on the workings of firms in socialist economies, which he hopes will provide more opportunities to attempt to practice what he preaches in this essay.

Writing is not something that economists spend much time thinking about let alone writing about, so this is a somewhat unusual exercise for me. Nevertheless, I have increasingly come to realize that my writing of economics plays a critical role in my doing of economics. Moreover, since it is generally true that the process of carrying out research is bound up with the writing up of the research, this connection is explored below, as it applies to researchers like me and to students, both graduate and undergraduate. Before doing so, however, we need a bit of background about the varieties of economic writing.

The main thing to know about economic writing is that it runs the gamut from technically oriented papers, overrun with Greek symbols and intelligible only to professional economists, to literate essays, unburdened by symbolism, at least of a mathematical sort, and understandable to a wide audience. To an extent, this range reflects research tastes and talents in that some of my colleagues only do economics that is heavily laden with mathematics and statistics, while others prefer more conventional and less formidable tools.

These days, however, most economists will have spent a good bit of their time doing technical research so, to a greater extent, the range of economic writing reflects the intended audience and not the proclivities of the author. In my own case, the audience has variously been my fellow economists, students, political or business practitioners, or the public at large. Correspondingly, the vehicles have been papers in professional journals, technical monographs, research proposals to foundations, a textbook, prepared testimony before Congressional committees, and the occasional piece in a magazine. Through two stints in government service I have also had occasion to write memos for political types, including the President, where clarity and, perhaps even more importantly, succinctness are critical. Since the importance of writing when addressing nonprofessionals is rather obvious, I will focus on the role of writing at the more technical end of the spectrum.

Many economists in the early stages of their research career tend to view writing as a necessary evil. It is necessary to avoid perishing, or more precisely to do publishing, but it is evil because it is not viewed as part of the research process. Moreover, since beginning economists have had relatively little experience in writing, the mechanics of their writing tends to be painful and time consuming. I know these views and ailments afflicted me in the early stages of my career and I have seen them present in many others as well.

As a result, newly minted economists who are so afflicted, and who by training are inevitably big on the notions of opportunity costs and budget constraints, tend to see writing as something that positively interferes with doing research.[1] For such individuals this has two consequences. First, they tend to wait until the

---

[1]Scarcity of resources is one of the big concepts in economics. If a scarce or constrained resource is not used in its most productive manner, then an opportunity cost is incurred. Aside from leading them into misguided attitudes toward writing, economists also get into trouble when

research is "finished" before beginning the writing process, and second, they tend to downplay the importance of polishing the writing.

This view is misguided on two counts. For one, even if writing made no contribution to research, how one writes up research can have a noticeable effect on the reputation of the researcher. To be sure, this effect is less pronounced where the bulk of the material is highly technical in nature, but even with technical material it is my distinct impression that better writing increases the speed with which new ideas get absorbed into the mainstream.

A more important reason why this view is misguided is that, strange as it may have seemed to me in the early stages of my career, writing is actually a critical part of the research process. With hindsight, the reasons for this seem so self-evident that it never ceases to amaze me how slowly I learned this lesson. Writing up one's results, whether analytic, empirical, or statistical, invariably serves to clarify some aspect of the research. It may reveal a hidden assumption or uncover some logical flaw in a mathematical argument or lead to the realization that some statistical approach or computer program is being inappropriately applied. Alternatively, the writing process may lead to bold new insights that substantially improve the research or lead to further topics for research (and more writing!).

I realize it is somewhat difficult to convey the sense of self-discovery that writing up research may produce, but I believe it works because the writing process becomes a vehicle for the researcher to step away from the research and examine it with something like a fresh eye. I find similar kinds of insights when I have to exposit to a class some theory that I am generally familiar with but have not really gotten into my bloodstream. I believe the same logic applies to student writing as a source of understanding. In this regard, I was recently struck by reports of a growing movement to require frequent writing exercises in courses in mathematics and physics at both the high school and college levels. According to reports, one student in a college math course that required writing concluded, "I never realize how

they try to apply these ideas in a household setting as in "my time is too valuable" to (a) mow the lawn, (b) take out the garbage, (c) wash the car, or (d) all of the above. Rational as these arguments seem to me, for some reason they are generally not well received.

little I understand until I try to write about it, and then when I have written about it, I realize how much I have learned."

Of course in both the writing and teaching contexts, the process only works if the material is approached with a certain amount of self-discipline. As far as writing is concerned, I personally find my source of self-discipline in the fact that I know the final product will be circulated to my fellow economists. The prospect of baring my intellectual soul to my peers tends, as a hanging is reputed to do, to focus my mind.

The moral of this for the researcher is that writing should occur at a relatively early stage in the research process, at least earlier than my, and I suspect most other's, natural inclinations. I confess, however, that it is easier to posit this dictum than to live by it. Many is the time that I am tempted to try one more mathematical manipulation or one more computer run, in the hope that some objectionable feature of the results, as they then stand, would be eliminated. The amount of time one can spend by trying just one more idea is quite extraordinary.

How much simpler matters usually are on those occasions on which I practice what I preach and force myself to write up my interim findings. As a consequence of starting at the beginning, and because my need to focus on the mechanics of writing forces me to stop spinning my wheels, I frequently find that the process yields an idea that helps to remove the objectionable feature, or finds others of which I was unaware. I would be too much of a Pollyanna, however, if I suggested that this always solves all technical problems, but I have never regretted plunging ahead with the writing. Since the writing has to be done at some point, at the worst, one is forced to put it aside until the requisite insight rescues the research from its inadequacies.[2]

There would seem to be a corollary to the principle of writing early in the research process: one should not be overly concerned with polishing the prose. After all, if the main purpose of early writing is to improve the research and if, as seems likely, the later versions of the research will necessitate some substantial

---

[2]There is, of course, the unpleasant possibility that no insight will be forthcoming and the research will remain in a permanently unpublishable state. In such a case the writing effort will have been undertaken needlessly. My own personal experience suggests that the expected benefits of writing to aid the research exceed the expected costs of needless writing. (You are probably wondering—Do economists really talk and think like this? Unfortunately the answer is yes.)

rewriting, why bother to fine-tune the text. If anything, I find this dictum even harder to follow than the basic idea that one should write early. There is something about an imperfectly expressed thought that demands my attention, and this attention inevitably takes longer than I expect. On those occasions when I muster up enough self-control to quit fussing, I invariably end up ahead in the long run, but these occasions are all too rare.

Another way around these issues is to do joint work with someone whose style it is to write up research at an early stage. This is, in fact, how a substantial fraction of my research has been done. Indeed, I have co-authored two books and over twenty-five papers with a single colleague who writes early and quickly. In about three-quarters of the cases he has taken responsibility for the first draft and I have been the fixer, a task for which my attention to detail and penchant to fuss is well suited. It is a relationship that has been productively enjoyable and has served us both well. In the absence of such good fortune, however, the principles outlined above should not be ignored.

If, as I have suggested, it takes some considerable experience to learn the virtues of writing as a research tool, what of the poor graduate student attempting a first piece of serious research in the guise of a doctoral thesis. Typically, the unwillingness to begin writing until the research is "done," coupled with the severe graduate student disease of self-criticism, combine to drag out the dissertation phase well beyond the bounds of decency and self-interest.

To understand the problem, one needs to realize that much of graduate education in economics consists of critical analyses of articles that have appeared or are about to appear in the leading professional journals. While this is a good way to learn about a wide variety of approaches, mathematical models, and statistical techniques, it tends to make graduate students such good critics that when they turn these skills on themselves the result is something akin to intellectual paralysis. They are capable of seeing the slightest imperfection in any of their own ideas and, remembering the critiques of the classroom, they are unwilling to expose themselves to what they anticipate will be public abuse.[3] So the quest goes on interminably for the perfect idea. Superimposed on this is the standard reluctance to write up

---

[3] Some years ago our department ran a seminar that encouraged graduate students to present work in progress as a way of speeding up the

incomplete research, and we have a recipe for a six-year doctoral process.

My personal experience in writing a doctoral dissertation was considerably shorter and less painful, although largely for extraneous reasons that are not easy to recreate. It was the early 1960s and a time in which academic jobs were plentiful. Indeed, I had secured a job in December for the following academic year with virtually nothing in the way of a dissertation to show prospective employers. For the next four or so months I was chained to the computer doing my research but without writing a word. Toward the end of May my wife went into the hospital to give birth, and I suddenly panicked with the realization that with her reappearance with our daughter, quiet time to write would be a scarce commodity. During the five days she was away (standards have changed!) I experienced the most productive period of my life, before or since, and managed to write 100 pages (with pencil and paper no less) and read James Michener's *Hawaii*. I suspect in some way the fact that this story had a happy ending contributed to my initial attitude that writing followed research rather than being an integral part of it.

While I have occasionally seen extraneous circumstances motivate our graduate students to bouts of feverish writing, reticence in writing is considerably more common. I encountered this in one of the first theses I supervised, with an extremely bright but diffident and somewhat insecure student. He seemed to think he would be wasting my time if he presented a less than perfect draft. His insecurity also led him to a fear of stating what to him was the obvious. Of course, what was obvious to him was not necessarily obvious to someone else, and consequently his writing tended to be quite cryptic. This story too has a happy ending and he is now a prominent and widely cited economist who with time and badgering by his colleagues has developed a rather wry and quite engaging style of writing.

Once the student does start writing other problems crop up. There is a general tendency to try and exhibit how smart you are by including all creative thoughts, even those only vaguely

doctoral process. Critiques were provided by both faculty members and fellow graduate students with the latter invariably providing the harsher comments. Indeed, a few bitter and painful exchanges led to a rather prolonged lapse in the seminar. In recent years several versions of these seminars have flourished and civility has prevailed.

related to the topic being discussed. Sometimes these distractions appear directly in the text, but the extraordinary abundance of footnotes in dissertations is also a result of this predilection. It is only with experience that we come to realize that sometimes more is less. Overall, however, given the difficulty of getting graduate students to write in the first place, these are problems that I happily put up with.

Perhaps, like adolescence, the long thesis gestation period is inevitable and no amount of mucking about will alter the process, but I periodically try. When I do, what I tell our graduate students is the following: most importantly, one should get out of one's head the idea that a dissertation needs to be or even can be perfect. Put somewhat weaker, a dissertation should not be thought of as one's magnum opus—how depressing it would be if it were. Put more weakly still, a dissertation is not even likely to be one's last word on the subject. Indeed, if my experience is any guide, within six months of completing a dissertation, one is quite likely to be unhappy with some aspect of the treatment, no matter how perfect the dissertation may have seemed at the time. Moreover, during the course of their professional lives most economists return again and again to the topic of their dissertation. This was certainly true in my case as well.

So while the first part of my pep talk to thesis writers emphasizes that a dissertation is not the quest for the Holy Grail, the second part emphasizes the importance of writing at an early stage. In fact, to those students who are primarily working with other faculty members I recommend that they take a quite aggressive approach to their advisors by marching in with a draft and asserting that they think they are done. (The role of self-control in avoiding polishing the text is particularly important here because the advisor may have some strong views on what should or should not be included.) While this rarely gains immediate acquiescence, the advisor is usually stunned 'y the audacity and over the longer haul is likely to prove more pliable. This comes about because, if the truth be known, it is not always well defined when a dissertation is done. As a consequence, if the student, having asserted that the thesis is finished, now demands to know what remains to be done, the list will likely to be shorter than would otherwise be the case.

Finally, I turn to the writing of economics by undergraduates. Princeton University, where I teach, requires at least two written research papers for juniors and a year-long thesis project for seniors. Over the twenty-five years I have been at Princeton I have supervised some 200 of these projects and received an ample supply of raw inputs, sometimes disturbingly raw, which cried out for some assistance in shaping into a finished product. Curiously enough, at the undergraduate level the reluctance to write is generally not a major issue, at least at first. Indeed, if anything, there seems to be an eagerness to write, whether or not the substance of the research warrants it. Perhaps not surprisingly, the major difficulty is communicating to the student just what constitutes an original research paper.

The problem is that, at least at first, many of our students equate research with going to the library and reading all they can on a particular topic. When they have mastered the material they are ready to write, whether or not they have an original idea to contribute to the subject. Academic researchers, on the other hand, are more confident that they know what the unsolved problems are and consider this the area of research. It is only when the original contribution is completed that they worry about the niceties of relating their research to previous work.

This difficulty is sufficiently widespread and well recognized that we make a special effort to overcome it. In particular, at the beginning of the junior year we give a number of lectures on what is expected in a research paper and how one goes about choosing a topic, giving ample examples of topics that have worked well in the past. For some students this is sufficient, but for others the substance of these lectures needs repeating, sometimes several times, on a one-to-one basis.

In any event, armed with the experience of the junior year our students then launch into their senior thesis. Perhaps as a result of the junior-year critiques, the reluctance to write increasingly rears its head, but the problem of what constitutes a research paper is still an issue for many.[4] As a result, for a substantial number of students, the thesis is a painful process,

---

[4]If the criticism of junior papers does explain a growing reluctance to write early, it is not because of the low grades we mete out. Indeed, there is evidence of embarrassing grade inflation for junior papers, inflation that disappears on the senior thesis. I believe the generous junior grades are due to the fact that advisors, after dealing with a student on an individual basis for a semester, find it distasteful to be harsh. While the same effect is present for senior theses, each thesis is read by a second faculty member, and this knowledge keeps us all a bit more honest.

especially in the early stages. What appears most critical in over-coming the initial hurdle is being enthused about the topic.

Perhaps the most vivid example of this was a recent student who frequently wrote long, amusing, well-written, and erudite articles for a campus publication on a subject in which he was passionately interested—baseball. Indeed, his consuming interests in both writing and baseball occasionally got him into academic difficulties, despite his considerable intellectual abilities. In fact, he was required to take a leave of absence from school, and he returned in the middle of his senior year faced with the prospect of a senior thesis.

After some discussion, he chose a topic that vaguely appealed to him but not enough so to spark a serious amount of work. Less than a month before the thesis was due, when it became apparent that the topic was no longer feasible, we managed to find a baseball-related topic of considerable economic interest. He had earlier rejected searching for a baseball topic, thinking it too self-indulgent and worrying about whether he would do too much baseball and not enough economics. Once armed with his new topic he was a sight to behold. He painstakingly gathered original data, taught himself the needed statistical techniques, carried out the research, and did a good job of writing it up, all in the space of three weeks. With a bit more work, the final product could well have been published in a professional journal. All in all, for him it was a quite satisfying, if hectic, experience.

While the details of this story are rather unique, the end result is not in that the painful senior thesis process appears on the whole to be an extremely satisfying one for most of our students. I suspect this is in part because of the sheer satisfaction of completing such a seemingly monumental undertaking and in part because students earn the satisfaction of mastering some subject to which they feel they have brought some original insights. Whatever the reason, surveys of graduating seniors and of alumni, both recent and of old vintage, invariably strongly support keeping the thesis as a requirement for all. Indeed, at the faculty symposia held for alumni when they return to campus, it is not uncommon to encounter an alumnus who wants to engage the faculty in a discussion to see what the current state of thinking is on his or her thesis topic. Somehow, I guess the process must be working.

16

On Writing My
Way Home:
Finding My Authentic Self
Within the Academy

LINDA WILLIAMSON NELSON

Linda Williamson Nelson was born in 1947 in the Bronx, New York. She is now an Assistant Professor of Writing at Stockton State College in southern New Jersey, where she teaches courses in writing, anthropology, and African-American literature and culture. She is currently writing a dissertation in anthropology that examines cultural themes and code shifting in oral life narratives of African-American women. She lives in Sicklerville, New Jersey, with her husband, her two children, two dogs, two cats, and a hamster.

When Mrs. Turner announced that our fifth-grade class at P.S. #58 in the South Bronx would have a book report contest, I decided I would win. As I remember it, the winner would be the one who read the most books. Since quantity was what counted, I decided to develop a strategy of alternating big books and little books, so that *Babar, the Elephant* and *Curious George* would hopefully go undetected among *Little Women, Treasure Island,* and *Adventures of Huckleberry Finn.*

Although I had received my share of A's in "English Expression," I went straight to the book jackets. My intention was not to copy the words but to listen to their cadence, because I knew that those words were different from my own. To this ten-year-old writer, the language of the jackets was smooth, precise, and even magical. I knew as well that the "jacket voice" was an outside voice, of school books and news reports, and not at all like the talk of 177th Street and Bathgate Avenue where I lived. Yet, I must have caught the cadence and some degree of specificity. I can't remember now if I won the contest, but I did learn a passable approximation of the "jacket voice."

Throughout grade school and high school I continued to go after recognition for "writing well," as I viewed it. This meant combining the "jacket voice" with my mother's starched Jamaican English, a tribute to the success of *her* mother's warnings against the use of the creole of the lower class which, as mother told it, "vexed the elders to no end."

But I was always keenly aware of other voices. Like an intimate longing, there was the voice of my father, a Mississippi sharecropper, who spoke to us sparingly in meandering folktales of talkin' alligators in swamps, of cullud boys making they way through graveyards at dusk, and of my great grandfather, a runaway slave who "nare one heard tell of sence." My father's voice was more like the voices of the parents, aunts, and uncles of my friends, as it spoke to me through the chords of his blues songs, from a cheap acoustic guitar and a small, metal harmonica. This was a rich, deep, tonal voice, a voice that was more metaphoric than literal, more hyperbolic than precise. Although overpowered by the "jacket voice," my father's voice has spoken to me all my life, but only in recent years has it vied against the standard of the academy to find resonance in my writing.

In schools, this vernacular held no sway, and in most black homes, the sentiments were not much different. My brother and sisters and I, who had learned to speak at Mother's knee, knew not to copy the way my father spoke except in child-play whispers, for it was clearly mother who seemed to have the power in her words. It was she who could talk to white people and make them listen. It was she who would intercede with school teachers on our behalf, negotiate credit with the corner grocery store owner, and reestablish our collective dignity when the home relief investigator questioned us to the point of humiliation. Before these forces, my father was silent, yet I think I suspected then, what I would later learn without question—that the music in his words and the larger-than-life pictures that they constructed were valuable currency somewhere.

I continued, however, to pattern my writing on the books and language of the classroom, while the speech of kitchen table and street corner discourse remained a subtle but enticing echo. And it worked. I was rewarded for my "good grammar and diction." My tenth-grade teacher encouraged me to send stories and poems to Junior Scholastic contests, while my weekly essays went on a hallway bulletin board. I was aware of a comforting feeling of being able to put the words together "right." That meant producing the appropriate amount of complex sentences and what I believed to be sophisticated sounding words for each assignment. Writing, for me then, was an act of conformity rather than an act of invention, which mirrored the truth of my experience.

Personal truths are hard to make on a page that is committed to a rigid sense of academic diction and prescribed subjects. The writing exercises that I received from the many Mrs. Turners demanded more than correct form: they required a neatly organized package of values and beliefs that stayed close to the traditional American myths of social equality, unimpeded upward mobility, and the incorruptible goodwill of most people. The repertoire of topics called for laundered news about personal goals, family life, favorite pastimes, and summer vacations. What I knew best through those early years was Dad's daily departure from our cold-water flat to look for work, but what I wrote was that he was self-employed as a house painting contractor. When I should have been describing the long afternoons I spent exploring vacant lots, I elaborated on trips to the zoo or the circus and of family picnic feasts in Central Park. Our actual feasts were five of us kids sitting Indian-style on the living room linoleum eating rice and beans and neckbones while my father gave us guitar concerts of his down-home improvisations called "Spanish Fling-Ding" and "Mississippi Back Road Boogie-Woogie." But the classroom texts gave me no indication that it was possible to write about a world without smiling blond-haired kids and neatly manicured lawns. My writing was never a conscious act of censorship. It was, however, a careful fabrication: my best words, revealing my clearest understanding of the way I believed everyday experience ought to have been.

I don't know that I could have written differently at the time, but I was aware of an undefined sense of conflict with the kitchen table voices of my culture. I didn't know then about the natural link between people's language and cultural experiences, but I did sense that the spontaneous images and tonal contours of black speech made it vibrant and bold. The conflict, as I see it now, came from intuiting that I belonged to two very different, even opposing, linguistic traditions, and that one was acceptable on the outside and that the other was not.

I wrote my way through undergraduate and graduate school only to find that as a teacher of writing and as a writer, the other voices continued to amplify, sometimes menacingly. But I kept them in check. In spite of—or maybe because of—this background chorus I, like many of us from marginal groups who enter academe, often overdo the requirements for acceptance. This tension is illustrated dramatically by the difficulty I found when asked to submit a brief, two- to three-paragraph description of what I would write about in this very essay. I was asked to keep the voice personal, so I began:

Tentative title: On Writing the Authentic Self within the Public Academy

> *The start of my composing process, that prearticulate shifting of ideas in the head, forces into conflict two seemingly opposing voices. Each voice is artifact, a range of linguistic signs and stylistic possibilities, that reflects one of the many layers of my enculturation. Each has given me in its turn a discrete form of articulatory power, negotiable in mutually exclusive arenas. . . .*

Only after the intervention of two patient colleagues and ten pages of revision did I accept that this was not my personal voice. Finally, I let go to write the abstract partially reproduced below:

> *If I write about the influence of my writing on the teaching of writing, I will have to begin with the self-consciousness and the tension that I feel long before I sit at my desk and pick up the pen. . . . The problem comes for me (and I can feel it even now as I write this) when I read out loud what I have just written and I can't hear a*

trace of the intimacy and sway of the Black vernacular that just a while ago spoke to me. Letting go of the "homegirl" voice would not, in itself, be a problem if it didn't also feel like at least a partial loss of my true self.

I know I am not the only one who struggles with this uncertainty. Marilyn Mobley, a black scholar best known for her work on Toni Morrison, describes it this way:

We are not always aware of how enlightened other people are, whether they will appreciate our use of the vernacular or the informal voice as strategy, or hear it as error. Among folks we know, white or black, we don't worry. In other settings, we are on guard; we are concerned about being judged. We have to be articulate, to be better than the best, lest they think we don't have full command over scholarly discourse. However, we are quickly approaching that place where we don't care how we are judged. But it's that kind of schizophrenia.

When I decided to focus my dissertation on the oral and written narratives of African-American women, the dilemma came to a head. Because I am writing about a disenfranchised community to a privileged audience of intellectuals within the academy, I finally had to reconcile the ongoing conflict between the voice of Mrs. Turner's books and the voice of the community of my enculturation. My colleagues are anthropological linguists, but the life stories of my informants are about marginalized African-American women, who challenge the belief system of the academy and the words I have learned to describe that system. The question of how to tell their stories authentically gives up no easy answers.

My solution has been to mediate between responsibility to my academic audience, and to my subjects, so I recognize the power of the vernacular. For example, in describing these women's sense of responsibility for the progress of the race, and to any member involved in this cause, I wrote,

These women, for the most part, were willing to assist me, a native researcher, as they believed that I was doing more than pursuing my personal research to enhance my career. My work was viewed instead as an effort that would ultimately contribute to the collective

progress of the entire race. Helping me, therefore, was seen as their
contribution to the larger cause.

However, I follow this generalization written in academic prose
with their actual voices, letting the women, like Miss Esther,
speak for themselves:

I believe in tryin to help somebody, one of us, if they help them-
selves, but if you don't try to help yourself, you'a lost soul and I
don't care to waste no time.

Or, as a Philadelphia mental health administrator told me as I
was leaving her office after our first meeting:

Yeah, girl, white folks always be studying us; we got to help each
other; we have to network.

By bringing their voices to my text as I heard them, I think my
academic writing comes alive with the vitality of truth that I've
missed for so many years.

There are a number of writers who have succeeded in this
way by mediating between the formal academic voice and the
vernacular of their people. Black anthropologist John L. Gwaltney skillfully weaves the voices of his subjects into his discussion
of core black culture in *Drylongso.* Sociolinguist Geneva Smitherman brings the power of the oral black language to the ex-
plication of her thesis in *Talkin and Testifyin.* And in the article
"The Black Writer and the Magic of the Word," John Wideman
writes eloquently of his own homecoming to black language use
in fiction, which for him is a rediscovery of "the primal authority
of your experience, experience whose meaning resides in the
first language you spoke."

Many of my students, not only the African-Americans, come
to my classroom with a chorus of family voices telling them what
they know, who they are, and what they believe in. While every
occasion to write does not usher in these private voices, some
invariably do, and some pieces of writing are made all the more
compelling by their use. My goal is to help students, whatever
they speak at home, develop confidence and skill to use *all* the
language that makes up their experience. For this, they must
know the differences between standard and non-standard English *and* be able to use either or both, depending on their rhe-

torical needs. I see this as a double responsibility as their teacher. To help those who are still unsure of the patterns of standard English, I teach the recurring patterns of non-standard use (such as the use of uninflected verbs and unmarked plurals among some African-American student writers) and show them contrasts between their constructions and standard ones. I also show them—as well as those who have mastered standard English—where in the context of their essays powerful cultural metaphors, such as the black student's "And God don't love ugly," can and should be saved. Finally, I stress peer review, for it provides the opportunity for all my students, including mono-dialectal standard English users, to experience voice diversity firsthand in the writing of their classmates. In this way, my students, hopefully, will learn to mediate among the various demands placed upon them as writers and will find their way home—taking *detours* with confidence.

If I am honest with the reader, I am not sure whether I have fully achieved the reconciliation of private self and public voice that I suggest in my title, especially if that implies a permanent privileging of one voice over the other. Many writers, particularly academics who work out of two opposing language traditions, have done this, and frankly, I don't like them much. Something powerful is missing. Instead, I prefer to keep struggling with my many voices—although sometimes... I just get bodacious and let the truth be told, even if it challenges the way some think it ought to be.

WORKS CITED

Gwaltney, John L. *Drylongso: A Self Portrait of Black America*. New York: Vintage, 1981.

Mobley, Marilyn S. Personal Conversation, August 1989.

Smitherman, Geneva. *Talkin and Testifyin*. Boston: Houghton Mifflin, 1977.

Wideman, John. "The Black Writer and the Magic of the Word." *New York Times Review of Books* 24 January 1988.

Thanks to Pamela Kennedy, Michael Robertson, Mimi Schwartz, and Neal Tolchin for responding to various drafts of this essay.

17

Anxious, B-L-O-C-K-E-D, and Computer Phobic: A Writing Teacher's Memoirs

ANDREA W. HERRMANN

Andrea W. Herrmann teaches writing with computers, sociolinguistics, and the art of teaching writing at the University of Arkansas at Little Rock. She also directs the MA program in technical and expository writing. Recent publications include, "Computers in the Public Schools: Are We Being Realistic?" in **Critical Perspectives on Computers and Composition Instruction** *and "Computers and Writing Research: Shifting Our 'Governing Gaze' " to appear in* **Computers and Writing: Theory, Research, Practice.** *When not writing—or trying to write—she travels with writer/editor husband, John, reads biographies, and photographs nature.*

One of my thesis writers jubilantly announced to me the other day that he had overcome a writing block. He was now writing well. I didn't realize he'd been blocked. "What did you do?" I asked.

"I've given myself permission to eat whatever I want," he

beamed, "until the thesis is written." He couldn't have shown more pride if he'd made a new translation of the Rosetta stone. Eating neurotically apparently was new to him, although this is something I've been doing for years. I was happy for his break-through but demoralized to discover that I had failed to share such an important insight.

Of course, I have never admitted my own eating/writing dis-order to anyone; even my husband doesn't know. Normally, I am a sensible, low fat, high fruits and vegetables, eater. That is, when the writing goes well. When blocked, the culinary rules change. For example, today since 9:30 A.M., when I began strug-gling to write this essay, I have eaten six large chocolate chip cookies (defrosted in batches of two in the microwave), one heavi-ly salted hardboiled egg, and three slices of toast smothered in strawberry jam. I have drunk several cups of herbal tea, includ-ing a cup of sweetened ginseng—for memory and energy—and a cup of hot chocolate.

By 1:51 P.M. I have eaten the cupboard bare and now must take a shopping break to lay in supplies for the remainder of my writing day. I will buy "finger food" that permits me to eat with one hand and keyboard with the other.

It occurs to me that I have never revealed these rituals to my students; in fact, I have never taught many of these fundamental lessons I learned as a writer. My feelings of inadequacy as a teacher now lead me to feel increasingly impotent to carry out this writing task. B-L-O-C-K-E-D. (I spell this so the writer in me doesn't *hear* it.) Yet I have not always experienced writer's block.

When I first became a professional ghost writer, writing under the name Alix Watson, I was never blocked. Ghost writing was easier for me than writing under my own name. This gave me permission to take risks. If something didn't work, what did I care? *I* wouldn't suffer the consequences, *Alix* would. It was the mid-fifties and I was an eighth-grade pupil at Belleview Junior High in Syracuse, New York. My sister—the real Alix Watson—was in the eleventh grade at Central High. While driving my father's 1953 lemon MG TC sports car, Alix discovered the fast lane. Her mounting obligations to boys, cheerleading, and so-rority left no time for homework.

One fall afternoon, Alix came home in a panic. "You've got to write a paper for me," she said. "For Miss Moran."

Miss Moran loved writers. And Alix, a promising writer, was her pet. "I've got sorority tonight. The paper's due tomorrow."

"Don't be absurd," I replied.

"I'll pay you a dollar. Come on. I only need two or three pages. You can do it."

"$3.00."

"Okay, $3.00. But it better be good. And make it long—and funny. She likes funny."

I tried to write long and funny about juggling two dates in one evening, something Alix once had tried to do and failed. I had nothing to lose; the writing flowed. In the morning Alix read it. She laughed, gave me $3.00, and then copied the paper over, fixing spelling and punctuation. Apparently Miss Moran laughed; she gave the paper an A. I was delighted to have the last laugh—or so I thought. I was delighted to be the family's comedy writer. For that year and the next, I churned out $3.00 essays for Alix and Miss Moran, and enjoyed my life as a hack.

Alix graduated, I arrived at Central as a sophomore, and as luck would have it, Miss Moran became my teacher. "Whatever you do, don't get on her bad side," Alix warned me. "She will make your life unbearable." A short, squarish woman with a ruddy complexion, cropped hair, and mannish clothes, Miss Moran sat spread-eagled behind her frontless desk while thirty-five students strained to see up her skirt but still pay attention.

Her first assignment, predictably, was to write a long, humorous essay. Winning over Miss Moran would be a cinch. But two days after turning in the assignment a stern-faced Miss Moran called me to the front of the room. I trembled so, my elbows shook. "I had great hope for you," she said, her lips curled back. "But I have been most disappointed."

"Disappointed?" I asked, fearful my muse had left me.

"Don't be coy. You know what you did. I would never expect anyone, particularly Alix's sister, to stoop so low."

"Low?" Obviously, Miss Moran had discovered my ghosting. I attempted to formulate the best way to repay Alix.

"I'd know Alix's wonderful humor and style anywhere. You didn't write this assignment."

I fought to keep a smile from my face. Despite my distress, the irony of the moment was not lost on me. "But I *did* write it," I pleaded. "Honest."

Miss Moran was not convinced.

The next day she announced that everyone would have to write an in-class essay. "We'll see how well everyone writes *in class*," she said, shooting me a wicked smirk.

With clammy hand, I wrote.

Furiously.

I had only thirty minutes to be funny.

Given the circumstances, it seemed impossible. Yet the balance of the year—and as it turned out the next one, too—rode on the tip of my hysterically racing pen. "Just once more," I begged my muse, "let me be funny."

Writing had never been less fun.

The next day a contrite Miss Moran called me to her desk. "I apologize," she said, pulling me close to her. "Your paper was wonderful. So funny. Before this, I would never have believed two people could write so much alike."

"No kidding?" I said. "I've always admired the way Alix writes."

That early writing experience is only one of many that I have never "taught." I have also never revealed my computer aches and pains. Like many other writers, my writing process has been transformed by the use of word processing. Writing with a pencil or typewriter is as remote to me now as writing on clay tablets with a stylus. My enthusiasm has led me to teach all my students how to write with computers. I stress the ease of using this tool and the numerous positive benefits. I tell them how computers facilitate revision and editing and that computers take the pain out of writing. I know this is not entirely true. Yet I tell this white lie to get students engaged in using the machines.

I do not admit that I wrap hot towels around my neck while working, visit the chiropractor for adjustments, and receive regular massages to alleviate the pain caused by word processing. Some nights I find my arm numb from the shoulder to my finger tips, signs that my carpel tunnel syndrome (read "painful nerve in the wrist problem") is recurring. I mention none of this.

Of course, the physical discomforts pale when compared to the psychic pain I once experienced learning to use computers. I used to be phobic concerning all things mechanical and, by extension, computerphobic. I believed that men carried the gene to dominate the mechanical world, so when something didn't work, I grabbed the first male I saw to solve the problem. Only sheer grit, tempered by a dose of mid-life madness, helped me subdue the computer age. In truth, like a woman after childbirth,

I now have amnesia about the anguish of learning EMACS on the DEC 20 at Teachers College, Columbia University. Were it not for an essay I'd written back then, the tenor of those trying times would be lost:

> *I am caught in a web of nightmarish procedures. I have bouts of madness when instead of hitting 'Control D' to delete a character, I hit 'Control C' and snap myself out of EMACS and into an empty monitor. I lose ideas and concentration; the rhythm and flow of my writing is gone.*
>
> *In addition to the mechanical interruptions, the terminals are not always available in the user room when I am able to write. Also, I do not want someone to interrupt me to ask when I'll be finished. Or to shout hysterically, "Help me! I'm not a computer jock!" Even short breaks away from the terminal to the bathroom are difficult, since people pull up chairs and sit eagle-eyed waiting for me to logout. . . .*

After I purchased my own microcomputer, all these problems vanished. In the quiet of my house, the machine has become an automatic tool, as much an extension of my body as my pen. Of course, since I no longer write in a user room, I have found other distractions to help me not write. Clothes to wash. Floors to scrub. Papers to grade. . . .

Years ago, as a novice, skiing Verbier in the Swiss Alps, I skied through a cloud and, temporarily blinded, turned off the intermediate trail onto a black trail (read "expert"). When the fog cleared I found myself on the edge of a precipice, a straight drop down into oblivion. For two hours I dwelled on my fear and did not move. The solution, of course, was to flip my skis around and go back the way I'd come. But I was not accomplished at flipping around my skis, and the fear of tumbling into the abyss kept me rivetted to the spot. Eventually I did turn, I did fall, and I did save myself by planting my pole firmly into the snow. I learned not to dwell on the fear: to get on with it. This sounds like good advice for the blocked writer, including me.

So how did I break my block this time and get on with my writing? I gathered around me Joan Didion, E. B. White, Annie Dillard, R. V. Cassill, S. J. Perelman, and others, confronting their ideas and trying to find my own while I clipped my toenails and brushed my cats.

One nagging thought that continued to present itself was the conviction that I am not a writer: Real writers fight bulls or sip mint julips on a veranda. Real writers write stories, novels, and plays or, better yet, poems. Annie Dillard rescued me: "The essay can do everything a poem can do, and everything a short story can do—everything but fake it." She gave me permission to tell my truth.

I also saturated myself in Joan Didion. I read as a writer, listening for resonant chords to see what techniques I might adapt or steal. I marveled at Didion's ability to tease out the larger reality represented by her own stories.

My thinking and reading continued for several weeks with frequent interruptions to bounce ideas off my other self, writer and husband, John. I interspersed these conversations—sometimes they were arguments—with notes jotted hastily on yellow tablets that were left scattered around the house, ready for the next inspiration. I began to feel a growing calm, a strong sense that I had something to say again. I began to write. My self-confidence grew, as it had that day in the Alps. I thank the community of writers that helped pull me back from the abyss.

Yet I have never described this process of writing to my students. I have not explained to them the importance of believing in oneself during an uneasy incubation nor of weathering the early chaos. Why not? Yesterday I pondered the question of what I know as a writer versus what I teach, as I stood peeling an apple.

I was eating sensibly again, and gazing at the dogwoods in bloom through my kitchen window. I spied a ladder-backed woodpecker strutting on the rail, nervously looking for cats. His eyes met and locked on mine. He cocked his red capped head to the side as if to ask, "What happened to that bird feeder?" I looked guiltily at my apple. But as I surveyed the burgeoning woods, I imagined the trees teeming with tender bugs and my heart hardened. "Time to find your own groceries, my friend," I reminded him. No doubt he wondered at my cruelty. And it *was* easily within my power to grant his wish. Yet this was a time of plenty and providing for his needs might make him unable to cope.

I confront this same ambivalence and this same paradox, whether I am dealing with birds or students. I am both powerful and impotent in the face of their needs. Sometimes I can provide help. Sometimes I can't. Sometimes the most important lessons students must learn their own way. Some lessons I have learned as a writer, I believe wiser not to share. I hope they are idiosyncratic, transitory. Having to cope with the fear. The self-doubt. The frustration. The pain. Some students I suspect are having lots of fun. They feel confident. They are optimistic. Why spoil it for them right at the beginning?